BARTHOLOMEUS BREENBERGH

(1598 – 1657)

Joseph distributing corn in Egypt

Richard Verdi

The Barber Institute of Fine Arts, The University of Birmingham
29 October 2004 – 23 January 2005

Bredius Museum, The Hague
12 February – 1 May 2005

In loving memory of
Godfrey John Brooks

Front cover, frontispiece and pages 4, 5 and 7:
details from *Joseph distributing corn in Egypt*,
The Barber Institute of Fine Arts (No. 2)

Published and © Copyright 2004 by
The Trustees of the Barber Institute of Fine Arts
The University of Birmingham

© Copyright in the text 2004 Richard Verdi

ISBN 0-7044-2476-2
Richard Verdi

Project management by Peter Owen
Designed and typeset by P. M. Owen Advertising
Printed in England by West Heath Press

BARTHOLOMEUS BREENBERGH

Joseph distributing corn in Egypt

Contents

6   Preface

8   Acknowledgements

9   List of Lenders

9   Abbreviations

Bartholomeus Breenbergh

10   The Artist's Life

11   The Early Years

18   The History Paintings of the Late Years

23   *Joseph distributing corn in Egypt*

27   Its Later Influence

Works Exhibited

32   Paintings

52   Drawings

63   Prints

67   Selected Bibliography

68   Photographic Credits

Preface

The trajectory of Bartholomeus Breenbergh's career beggars belief. After serving an apprenticeship in the Netherlands, he moves to Italy in 1619, where he establishes a reputation as a masterly landscape draughtsman and as a painter of pastoral scenes featuring nymphs, shepherds and antique ruins. With his return to Amsterdam in about 1629 he increasingly introduces important historical subjects into his landscapes and then makes a brief incursion into portraiture and devotional painting before becoming a history painter, modelling his art on the immediate precursors of Rembrandt. His career finally culminates in a series of monumental figure pictures - including the Barber Institute's *Joseph distributing corn in Egypt* - which draw upon an even wider range of sources from the Italian and Netherlandish traditions. Throughout all of these transformations he remains essentially an outsider who scarcely engages with the art and ethos of the native Dutch school. In a land of specialists, he refuses to specialise, cultivating a wide range of subjects and styles from the art of the Renaissance and his own time that make him one of the most individualistic painters of his day.

This exhibition focuses on the Barber Institute's own masterpiece by the artist, which is an autograph replica of a picture of one year earlier. The two are here shown together for the very first time. Also included are a range of earlier landscape drawings and paintings by Breenbergh, to set his art in a wider context, and a selection of the most important history paintings leading up to the Barber Institute's picture. Pride of place among these is the frenetic - and cornucopian - *Martyrdom of Saint Lawrence* and a fine copy of the artist's earliest version of *Joseph distributing corn in Egypt* (now destroyed), which has good claims to be regarded as the most important work of his career, making the loss of the original canvas even more regrettable. Rounding off the display are pictures by two related masters, Johannes Lingelbach and Ferdinand Bol, which reveal the influence of Breenbergh's rare history paintings upon his contemporaries, and examples of yet another category of art at which Breenbergh excelled - etching.

The exhibition is the latest in a series centred on major masterpieces in the Institute's collection, one of which - *Matthias Stom, 'Isaac blessing Jacob'* (1999) - was also devoted to a little-known Dutch master. Like its predecessor, it is hoped that the present exhibition will greatly enhance the understanding and appreciation of an unjustly neglected artist, who is among the most diverse, inventive - and sheerly delightful - painters of the Dutch Golden Age.

Acknowledgements

In devising this exhibition, I have been acutely aware of the debt owed to those individuals and institutions who have helped to make it a reality. Foremost among these are the British Museum and National Gallery, London, the Städelsches Kunstinstitut, Frankfurt am Main, and those private collectors in Europe and the United Kingdom who have chosen to remain anonymous. Thanks are also due to the Bredius Museum, The Hague, for generously agreeing to give the exhibition a showing in Breenbergh's native land and to the RKD (Rijksbureau voor Kunsthistorische Documentatie) The Hague and, in particular, Edwin Buijsen for undertaking a technical examination of *Christ and the Centurion* at the last minute. I am additionally grateful to David Pulford and the staff of the Barber Fine Art Library for coping with my endless research requests, and to Paul Spencer-Longhurst, Senior Curator at the Institute, and Rosemary Poynton, Registrar, who has facilitated the practical realisation of the exhibition with her customary skill and efficiency. The industry and imagination of Peter Owen have ensured that the catalogue and supporting texts do Breenbergh the justice he deserves, and warrant my fullest appreciation. But my profoundest gratitude is reserved for Yvonne Locke and John van Boolen for their unswerving dedication to the project - and its author - during the most difficult of times and, especially, to Michael Walpole, who leapt in at a late stage in the exhibition's gestation - and made so much difference.

Richard Verdi
Director
The Barber Institute of Fine Arts,
The University of Birmingham

List of Lenders

De Nieuwe Kerk, Amsterdam, 11

The Bowes Museum, Barnard Castle, Co. Durham, 8

The Barber Institute of Fine Arts,
The University of Birmingham, 2

Städelsches Kunstinstitut, Frankfurt am Main, 9

Rafael Valls Ltd., London and Hoogsteder & Hoogsteder,
The Hague, 4

The British Museum, London,
13, 14, 15, 16, 17, 18, 19, 20, 21, 22, 24, 25, 26

The National Gallery, London, 6

Day & Faber, London, 12

Rafael Valls Ltd., London and Douwes Fine Art,
Amsterdam, 5

Belasting & Douane Museum, Rotterdam,
The Netherlands, 7, 23

Private Collection, Europe, 3, 10

Private Collection, United Kingdom, 1

Abbreviations

The following abbreviations are used throughout the catalogue:

Hind 1926   Arthur M. Hind, *Catalogue of Drawings by Dutch and Flemish Artists... in the British Museum, III, Dutch Drawings of the XVII century (A-M)*, London, 1926.

R1969   Roethlisberger, Marcel, *Bartholomäus Breenbergh, Handzeichnungen*, Berlin, 1969.

R1981   Roethlisberger, Marcel, *Bartholomeus Breenbergh, The Paintings*, Berlin and New York, 1981.

R1991   Roethlisberger, Marcel George, *Bartholomeus Breenbergh*, Richard L. Feigen & Company, London, 1991.

Bartholomeus Breenbergh

The Artist's Life

Bartholomeus Breenbergh was baptised in Deventer on 13 November 1598, one of at least eight children of a wealthy Protestant family.[1] His father, who was the town apothecary, died in 1607, whereupon the family moved, probably to Hoorn, 30 km north of Amsterdam. Nothing is known of the artist's apprenticeship, though it is assumed that he studied in Amsterdam, as his earliest works reflect the style of the Pre-Rembrandtists, a group of artists dominated by the future teacher of Rembrandt himself, Pieter Lastman (1583-1633), who resided there. Breenbergh was certainly in Amsterdam by October 1619, when he gave testimony and was already listed as a painter.

Later in the same year, the artist is recorded in Rome, where he was living with the painter Frans van de Kasteele and had already met the Flemish landscape master, Paul Bril (1554-1626), who was then in his sixty-fifth year and had resided in Italy since the early 1580s. Soon after, Breenbergh must also have met the Dutch landscape painter, Cornelius Poelenburgh (1594/5-1667), who was in Rome between 1617 and 1627, and with whose early works Breenbergh's would frequently be confused. Both men were among the founding members of the 'Schildersbent' ('band of painters') - or 'Bentvueghels' ('birds of a feather') - an association of Northern artists resident in Rome, which was founded in 1623. Little is otherwise known of his years in Italy, though the existence of a number of landscape drawings of views near Bomarzo and Bracciano, north of Rome, suggests that the artist enjoyed the patronage of Count Orsini of Bracciano during this period.

Breenbergh is believed to have returned to Amsterdam around 1629 and was certainly back there by 1633, the year in which he married Rebecca Schellingwou, who came from a family of merchants. The couple are presumed to be portrayed in two pendant portraits by Jacob Backer of c. 1644, which reveal their elevated social status (fig. 1 & 2).[2] Settling in the city for the rest of his life, Breenbergh is listed as a merchant in Amsterdam in 1652 and 1655. But he also continued to work as a painter; and, although his output diminished, his later works are among the most ambitious - and superlative - of his entire career. Changing residence several times during these years, he is recorded as living in the prestigious Herengracht in Amsterdam in 1657 and was buried in the Oude Kerk in the city on 5 October of that year. Though virtually ignored by seventeenth-century critics, he was much praised - and collected - by those of the succeeding century, especially in France, where many of his greatest works were then to be found - and where Dézallier d'Argenville characterised him in 1745 as a 'very spiritual' painter, capable of the utmost refinement and perfection in the depiction of animals and small figures.[3]

Breenbergh's surviving works consist of around 100 paintings, nearly 200 drawings and over 50 etchings. Though the majority of his drawings date from the Italian years, most of his paintings were executed after his return to the Netherlands. The latter are dominated by Italianate landscapes, often depicting historical themes, and betray a predilection for the bizarre and fantastic that was never to leave him. Around 1644, however, Breenbergh redirected his art dramatically towards the treatment of monumental themes dominated by the human figure. In these, landscape becomes increasingly subservient and his art assumes a hitherto unheralded grandeur and a new tone of high seriousness. This sudden conversion to a more elevated style of painting - and the motives that may have occasioned it - form the focus of the present exhibition, which centres around the supreme achievements of his later years, among them the Barber Institute's own *Joseph distributing corn in Egypt*.

The Early Years

Breenbergh's earliest dated work is his *Finding of Moses* (fig. 3) of 1622, painted when he was twenty-four years old and long past his apprenticeship.[4] As a Dutch artist of the seventeenth century, he is most likely to have served this in his mid teens, beginning around 1613-14 and lasting until 1618-19, when he was officially documented as a painter. But the identity of his teacher remains a mystery to which the *Finding of Moses* provides the only clues.

Set in a rocky and precipitous landscape, the picture depicts the familiar Old Testament subject enacted by a group of diminutive figures characterised by their gnarled and caricatural features, clinging draperies and (in the two women at the right) disproportionately small scale in relation to the main group. The closest analogies to this style among Breenbergh's contemporaries are in the art of Jacob Pynas (c. 1592/93-c. 1656), one of the

Fig. 1, Jacob Backer, *Bartholomeus Breenbergh*, Historisches Museum, Amsterdam

Fig. 2, Jacob Backer, *Rebecca Schellingwou*, Historisches Museum, Amsterdam

Pre-Rembrandtist masters working in Amsterdam in the second decade of the seventeenth century. Alone among this group of artists, Pynas - whose art suggests that he had visited Italy - specialised in both history paintings and landscapes, as Breenbergh himself would later do. The latter consisted of mountainous views with small, slightly ungainly figures derived from Paul Bril, with whom Breenbergh himself would be in contact in the early 1620s. Ultimately, however, both were indebted to the German master, Adam Elsheimer (1578-1610), whose protean art provided the chief source of inspiration for all of the Pre-Rembrandtists.

A painter of both history pictures and landscapes, Elsheimer spent much of his active career in Italy specialising in small, jewel-like works in which the monumentality of the classical tradition is combined with a vibrant colouring, a fascination with phenomenal light effects and a precision of handling that are northern in origin, as in the *Stoning of St Stephen* of 1603-4 (fig. 4). Much admired and collected by both Rubens and Rembrandt, he was also the abiding model for the latter's teacher, Pieter Lastman, who was already praised in a poem of 1618 for having helped to elevate the art of painting in Amsterdam to a position that rivalled even

Fig. 3, Bartholomeus Breenbergh, *The Finding of Moses*, 1622, Hallwylska Museum, Stockholm

12

that of Italy.[5] Given the later course of his development, there can be little doubt that this group of artists haunted Breenbergh's imagination for the rest of his career. But whether his earliest landscapes were directly inspired by Jacob Pynas in Amsterdam or his first encounter with Bril in Rome depends upon the chronology of the former's own works in this vein, which remains far from certain.

Few other paintings by Breenbergh may be securely dated to his Italian years; but, on stylistic grounds, around thirty other landscapes are attributable to this

Fig. 4, Adam Elsheimer, *The Stoning of St Stephen*, National Gallery of Scotland, Edinburgh

period, the majority depicting prominent Roman architectural ruins and remains, some of them identifiable. With rare exceptions, these are devoid of important historical subjects, suggesting that during his Italian years Breenbergh earned his livelihood executing idyllic views of the Roman Campagna unencumbered by weightier concerns.

More important than Breenbergh's early paintings are the more than 100 landscape drawings of his Italian years, many of which are signed and dated, suggesting that they were sold or commissioned and provided the artist with an important source of revenue. These are independent works of art, which are unrelated to his paintings and are executed in pen and brown or grey wash and frequently depict the ruins and architectural landmarks of the Campagna. In style they are vigorous and virtuosic, with lively pen work interspersed with bold passages of wash - as in the *Fountain of Pegasus at Bomarzo* (cat. 13) - and anticipate the landscape drawings of Breenbergh's two great successors in this field, Claude and Poussin. Many were clearly executed on the spot and possess a spontaneity and freshness that make them among Breenbergh's most enduring contributions to the Western landscape tradition. Nor did the artist abandon such imagery upon his departure from Rome. Long after he had resettled in Amsterdam he continued to draw imaginary landscapes of Roman ruins, a group of which formed the basis for a set of etchings he completed in 1639-40.[6] Thereafter, his paintings themselves continue to reveal a predilection for bizarre architectural motifs set in wild and dramatic landscapes and attest to Breenbergh's essentially romantic nature.

With his return to Amsterdam, Breenbergh entered the most prolific phase of his career, with no fewer than 70 paintings dating from the 1630s and early 1640s. In contrast to the works of his Italian years, a high proportion of these are signed and dated and exhibit one other fundamental difference from their predecessors. Whereas the vast majority of Breenbergh's

Italian landscapes contained no historical subjects, those that followed them usually do, drawing their themes from the Bible, mythology and other literary sources. Though the reasons for this sudden conversion to more momentous themes may never be explained - especially when nothing is known of Breenbergh's clientele - one likely reason is the popularity of the works of Pieter Lastman and his school, all of whom specialised in small historical paintings which were ideal for display in domestic interiors, where they might impart a moral lesson. When Lastman died in 1633, this style was perpetuated by Jacob Pynas and Claesz Cornelius Moeyaert (1590/91-1655). It may be that the master's death left a gap in the market that Breenbergh also helped to fill, but this is far from certain. For, with his marriage into a family of merchants in 1633, the artist possibly found himself provided with a greater measure of material comfort and less reliant upon his painting for an income, which would explain the steep decline in his output during his later years. If this was the case, the most plausible explanation for his shift towards more learned subjects would lie elsewhere: namely, in a desire to set himself fresh intellectual challenges.

Breenbergh's dated works of 1630 already reveal the dramatic changes in his style that accompanied his return to Amsterdam. In isolated paintings of this year he replaces his habitual Roman landscape with one which is more verdant and wooded (i.e. northern), portrays a New Testament subject in an upright format with an architectural (rather than a landscape) setting, and relegates an Ovidian subject to the middle distance of a picture, filling the foreground with a group of onlookers - a familiar mannerist device that will recur later in his career.[7] Since none of these innovations signals a permanent shift in the direction of his style, they must be seen as experiments, which reveal Breenbergh extending his own creative boundaries in ways that will ultimately transform his art.

A more decisive change that occurs in the artist's career at this time is his sudden predilection for larger, more complex and more animated figure groups - for crowds of figures re-enacting a drama in a landscape setting which, at times, seems a mere backdrop. In these, a fully-fledged history painter, in the mould of Lastman, appears to be asserting himself over the erstwhile master of the Roman Campagna.

Among the most ambitious works in this vein is the *Coastal Landscape with Saul after the Conversion* (cat. 5) of 1633, which portrays Saul on the road to Damascus after his divine revelation. Groping his way forward, still blinded by his vision, he is accompanied by his soldiers, who point him in the direction of the city, which lies nestled on the horizon at the right. In the transition between the sombre and precipitous landscape behind Saul and the ethereal beauty of his eventual destination, Breenbergh retraces the convert's spiritual journey from danger to safety - and darkness to light - with remarkable subtlety. Far from being a mere landscape painter, here is an artist both able and willing to deploy his skills in that field to the more demanding and ambitious art of storytelling.

Even more complex is another painting of these years, *Christ and the Nobleman of Capernaum* or *Christ and the Centurion* (cat. 4). Whereas the *Saul* depicts a procession of figures all headed in the same direction, this is a scene in which the cast of characters is more strikingly differentiated in pose and expression. The subject is that of the Roman nobleman whose faith in Christ was so steadfast that his ailing servant was miraculously healed by the Lord. Kneeling before him in an eloquent and intensely reverential manner, the nobleman gazes heavenwards as Christ turns to his disciples, marvelling at the nobleman's faith. Surrounding them is a group of onlookers whose subtly delineated reactions to the centurion's devoutness approach those of the history paintings and etchings of the young Rembrandt. Particularly moving are the rapt figures of the children, the bent old woman leaning on her stick, who appears mesmerised by the nobleman's words, and the wonderment and curiosity of the Pharisees and soldiers who gaze on in dawning recognition of the miraculous powers of Christ.

These tendencies are carried further in Breenbergh's *St John the Baptist preaching* (fig. 6) of 1634, which derives from a lost Lastman that was also to inspire Rembrandt to one of his most complex multi-figure pictures during these same years.[8] Breenbergh depicts a throng of onlookers listening to the Baptist's sermon - some attentively, others sceptically - while, in the background left, numerous figures go about their daily lives oblivious to the word of the Lord. But whereas Lastman sets his group before an enclosed landscape, both Breenbergh and Rembrandt locate it in a much more spacious and exotic realm of ancient ruins and distant mountains. This inevitably prompts one to wonder how much these two artists knew of each other's works during this period. One certain connection was their deep immersion in the richly inventive narrative painting of their predecessor, Pieter Lastman.

Although the landscapes with Saul and the Baptist reveal Breenbergh's burgeoning interest in history painting, their innovations were not immediately turned to account in his works of the mid-1630s, as the *Finding of Moses* (cat. 6) of 1636 makes clear. In this, Breenbergh's familiar, Lilliputian figures enact the biblical drama dwarfed by a spacious landscape of classical ruins, in the manner of the artist's works of the 1620s. But in another group of works datable to these same years, the artist paints four upright pictures virtually devoid of landscape and dominated instead by the monumental depiction of the human figure.[9] In one, the *Resurrection of Christ* (fig. 5), the drama is enacted with an explosive force that rivals that of Rembrandt, whose Passion pictures of the 1630s also adopt the arched top here employed by Breenbergh. Though this is probably no more than coincidental, it is yet another curious point of intersection between these two artists that one encounters in Breenbergh's later years.

The works of the early 1640s spring yet more surprises and include at least two exceedingly accomplished portraits, both signed and dated 1641, which clinch Breenbergh's position as one of the few Dutch seventeenth-century painters other than Rembrandt to refuse to confine themselves to a single specialism.[10] They are followed by a second *St John the Baptist preaching* (fig. 7) of 1643 that demonstrates the remarkable advances Breenbergh had made in his art since the panel of this subject of nine years earlier.

Fig. 5, Bartholomeus Breenbergh, *The Resurrection of Christ*, Art Institute of Chicago

Fig. 6, Bartholomeus Breenbergh, *St John the Baptist preaching*, 1634, Metropolitan Museum of Art, New York

The 1634 version depicts a large and essentially undifferentiated crowd of figures listening to the Baptist's sermon and, in the background, a welter of others engaged in everyday activities which provide a distraction - or, at least, a digression - from the main scene. In keeping with its transitional position in the artist's career, the work also contains a large and imposing landscape and effectively straddles two distinct categories in the hierarchy of subjects, in the manner of Pieter Bruegel the Elder's panoramic landscapes with religious themes of the 1550s and '60s.

In the 1643 version, the size of the figures is greatly increased and the landscape reduced and devoid of such eye-catching motifs as the ruin at the upper left of the earlier picture. The action itself is also more pointed and focused, with every pose, gesture and expression evidently the product of much thought. Whereas the 1634 picture depicts an anonymous crowd of listeners, the later work portrays distinct groups which explore the gamut of reactions to the Baptist's words. These include a pilgrim

Fig. 7, Bartholomeus Breenbergh, *St John the Baptist preaching*, 1643,
Private Collection, on loan to the Art Institute of Chicago

(far left) who has paused on his travels and sits on his donkey immersed in the Baptist's sermon and, on the opposite side, two Pharisees who dispute it. Between them Breenbergh explores a range of actions and reactions of remarkable psychological subtlety and virtually no duplication. Two mothers appear, each with an infant at her breast, a traditional symbol of charity. But whereas one is enraptured by the Baptist's words, the other is distracted by an elder child, who appears to be whining, and attempts to silence it. Around them figures doze, bury their heads in their hands, as though lost in thought, or simply listen attentively. To the centre left, a youth, maiden, turbaned man, and black boy gaze on in wonderment. Representing three ages of man, they are 'complemented' at the background left, where a group of elder scribes contemplate a sacred text, as though seeking confirmation of the Baptist's claims. But the masterstrokes of the picture are the figures of the Baptist himself and the nude youth seated in the centre foreground. In contrast to the protagonist of the 1634

17

picture, who waves his arm in the air seeking to win over his audience with sheer exhortation, the Baptist of 1643 articulates his words with a measured movement of his hands, explaining rather than exclaiming. And, although the reactions of the muscular youth in the foreground cannot be discerned, the inspiration for him probably can. He resembles traditional depictions of Lazarus, the beggar who appeared at the table of the rich man, where he was refused a morsel of food. As the Bible indicates (Luke, XVI, 19-31), it is the youth, and not his host, who will eventually find a place in the kingdom of heaven. With remarkable ingenuity, Breenbergh here approaches a level of symbolic allusiveness - and sheer learnedness - that one would simply not have expected from the uncomplicated nature of his earlier art. At this point in his career, he is a worthy successor of Lastman as a storyteller, and far surpasses his predecessor as a master of colour, light, and atmosphere.

The History Paintings of the Late Years

Nearly twenty dated paintings are known from the last fourteen years of Breenbergh's career and about another half dozen are assigned to this period by Roethlisberger. The majority are what one would expect from the artist: landscapes with historical subjects from the widest range of sources - the Bible, classical history and mythology and literature. It is hard not to regard this as indicative of an increasingly innovative artist, and this is confirmed by other aspects of the pictures of his later years. In many of these - such as *Amaryllis crowning Mirtillo* (cat. 8) of c. 1645 - the scale of the figures is substantially increased from that of the 1620s and '30s; and this change points towards the most momentous development to occur in the concluding phase of Breenbergh's career.

The chief masterpieces of these years are history paintings of a richness and complexity that the artist had never attempted before. In these, landscape plays no significant role and, instead, architecture forms the backdrop. When added to the intricate and ambitious figure groups placed in such settings, this makes these works the most austere and monumental of all the artist's creations and entitles Breenbergh to be regarded as a latter-day rival not only of Lastman, but even of Elsheimer. Perhaps it is no coincidence that he paraphrased works by both of these masters during the final years of his career.

What precipitated this change of direction in Breenbergh's art? In the absence of any knowledge of his patrons during this period, we can only guess. One reason might be the artist's increased financial independence, given that he now had another career as a merchant. This would account for the experimental nature of many of his late works, as also for the small number of these to survive from this period.

But Breenbergh's late - and sudden - foray into history painting may also have been prompted by opportunistic considerations, which are relatively easy to identify. During the third quarter of the seventeenth century, religious and historical pictures respectively commanded the first and third highest prices of all Dutch paintings, with architectural subjects sandwiched between them.[11] Thus, there can be no doubt as to their lucrative potential. This in turn may have been fuelled by the sudden market for such works which opened up during these same years for paintings for the newly-built Town Hall in Amsterdam. These were eventually to consist of a mixture of biblical and historical canvases on themes pertinent to the building's social and political roles, executed by a host of history painters that eventually included Rembrandt himself.[12] Was Breenbergh bidding to become one of these in his late incursions into this genre? It is impossible to say and, on the face of it, unlikely, as the scale of the pictures required for the Town Hall was far in excess of anything he had ever attempted. What will be seen in due course, however, is that his two compositions of Joseph distributing corn in Egypt exerted a major influence on the one canvas of this theme incorporated into the Town Hall and on a number of other such works by artists associated with it.

Breenbergh's late career begins in 1644 with a lost version of this theme (cat. 7), which portrays Joseph selling the corn that he has stored over seven good years to the Egyptians at a time of famine. Although still painted in a landscape format, the picture represents a radical departure from anything that had gone before it in the artist's career, even the *St John the Baptist preaching* of one year earlier. To be sure, the designs of the two works are closely connected, with the protagonist elevated above a crowd grouped around him, but in the earlier painting all of the figures ultimately relate to the Baptist; and, in this sense, the picture may be said to possess a single focus. In the *Joseph*, however, this is no longer the case, with the majority of the figures arranged in smaller, self-contained units and engaged in distinctive actions which encapsulate the gamut of responses to Joseph's beneficent act. Some are depicted bargaining with him, offering jewellery in exchange for corn, and others paying money for it, or gathering and carrying it off. Still others, seated around tables, collect payments for these rations or scrutinise their account books. Taken together these incidents - or episodes - aim to tell the entire story by showing its separate stages telescoped into a single scene.

The immediate inspiration for this picture was Pieter Lastman's painting of the same subject of 1612 (fig. 8), which became a touchstone for those of his followers treating the subject.[13] Breenbergh emulates Lastman in including an obelisk in the background, to locate the scene in Egypt, and in elevating Joseph above a chorus of figures exchanging their money or livestock for grain. But

Fig. 8, Pieter Lastman, *Joseph distributing corn in Egypt*, 1612, National Gallery of Ireland, Dublin

whereas Lastman concentrates upon the relieving of their hunger, Breenbergh pays equal attention to their plight. This aspect of the narrative is accentuated in three other depictions of the theme by Jan Pynas (1618) and Claes Cornelisz Moeyaert (1633 and 1644), the last of which (fig. 9) coincides in date with Breenbergh's lost picture.[14] Whichever came first (and who could possibly know?), it confirms the close relationship between the two artists while also illuminating the crucial differences between them. In Moeyaert's picture, all of the figures are grouped together in a huddled mass with Joseph appearing as merely one of them, standing at the top of a flight of stairs at the right as part of the crowd. In contrast, Breenbergh isolates Joseph through his frontal pose, commanding presence, parasol and - most importantly of all - the space around him. This may be said of all of the figures in the picture and distinguishes Breenbergh's treatment from those of the Pre-Rembrandtists. Hand in

Fig. 9, Claes Cornelisz Moeyaert, *Joseph distributing corn in Egypt*, 1644, present whereabouts unknown

of numerous copies and two reproductive etchings of the design (cat. 23 and 24). Admittedly, the prints were executed by the artist himself and by a close follower, who may have been his pupil. But it is worth remembering that such works were aimed at a commercial market.

In 1645-6, Breenbergh's style underwent a further transformation when he painted three history pictures in an upright format, among them *The Death of Abel* (fig. 11). Although the artist had occasionally employed this for such themes earlier in his career, he had hitherto used it for subjects which were wholly figural - such as the *Resurrection of Christ* (fig. 5) - or for those in which landscape was still the dominant element. But in the works of the mid-1640s, the figures are accorded much greater importance than their setting, and in none more

hand with this desire to provide breathing spaces - or caesuras - around his figures goes Breenbergh's rhythmic and harmonious grouping of them across the foreground of his picture. Here a sequence of interweaving poses arranged in a single, sinuous curve leads one seamlessly from the youth at the lower left to the camel and oxen at the far right.

In these respects, Breenbergh's painting invites comparison not with the works of his Dutch predecessors but with the heroic scenes of almsgiving, executed on a grand scale, which he could have seen in Italy. Among the most celebrated of these are Annibale Carracci's *Saint Roch distributing Alms* of c. 1595 (Gemäldegalerie, Dresden) and Domenichino's *St Cecilia distributing alms to the Poor* (San Luigi dei Francesi, Rome; fig. 10) of 1612-15, the latter of which Breenbergh must have known. With its carefully posed and articulated figures and its declamatory gestures and expressions, Domenichino's fresco treats the narrative with a loftiness and lucidity for which Breenbergh is clearly striving in his picture. That he was deemed successful in this is apparent from the existence

Fig. 10, Domenico Zampieri (Domenichino), *St Cecelia distributing Alms*, San Luigi dei Francesi, Rome

Fig. 11, Bartholomeus Breenbergh, *The Death of Abel*, 1645, Koninklijk Museum voor Schone Kunsten, Antwerp

so than the *Sacrifice of Elijah* (fig. 12), which takes its dramatic subject from I Kings XVIII, 16-39 and portrays a theme that the artist had treated eight years earlier in a landscape format.[15]

The upright composition of the second version was to be increasingly favoured by Breenbergh in his late history paintings and has numerous precedents which testify to the hybrid nature of his art. Though rarely employed by the Pre-Rembrandtists themselves, it was much used by their chief influence - Elsheimer - as by Rembrandt himself in the 1630s and '40s. Since Breenbergh paraphrases the former in another painting of these years, the *Martyrdom of St Stephen* of 1645,[16] Elsheimer is the more likely source, though it is worth noting that Dutch art generally came to favour the more stately and compressed upright format around the middle of the century.

Breenbergh's next dated history painting is his most ambitiously orchestrated of all. This is the *Martyrdom of St Lawrence* of 1647 (cat. 9), which contains his most elaborate figure group and reveals a near-manic inventiveness that appears intended to silence all critics who might have deemed him capable of producing nothing other than classical landscapes with miniscule figures. Set against an architectural background replete with Roman landmarks, the picture enlists the aid of a veritable army of figures to execute a single saint and displays so prolific a range of figural groups as had scarcely been seen in art since Pieter Bruegel the Elder and his followers. Incident is piled upon incident, and episodes multiplied, with an extravagance and theatricality that seem unstoppable and are strenuously held in place only by the crisscrossing diagonals that converge upon the figure of the saint.

Breenbergh's inexhaustible imagination here reveals him relishing the task of creating figures and actions that provide an encyclopaedic reconstruction of the martyrdom itself. Above the saint three sinister and demonic elders of the temple, worthy of Salvator Rosa, gesture admonishingly towards a statue of Mercury, symbol of the pagan world that Lawrence has forsaken, and which has occasioned his cruel fate. As vicious executioners stoke the flames, prodding the saint, a youth fans the fire from below. To the left of him, a muscular henchman prepares more wood for the pyre; while, behind him, a young boy bears another basket-load of it. In the background, myriad onlookers are held at bay by the Roman soldiers - crowd control at a public execution on a scale worthy of Hollywood, if not of Pandemonium itself. Amidst all this violence and mayhem, only the figure of St Lawrence strikes a somewhat discordant note, his sensuous and abandoned pose reminiscent at least as much of a recumbent odalisque as of a tormented saint.

The inventiveness of the *St Lawrence* was not achieved without a strenuous effort on the artist's part. For, in

Fig. 12, Bartholomeus Breenbergh, *The Sacrifice of Elijah*, 1645,
Statens Museum for Kunst, Copenhagen

designing this scene, he makes reference to a wealth of earlier works by artists from antiquity to his own day with a studiousness and receptivity that cannot fail to move the student of his art. Here - for whatever reason - is a painter who had concentrated on landscape for at least twenty-five years suddenly taking on the new and greater challenge of history painting in his fiftieth year, by apprenticing himself to the masters of this genre of his own time and earlier, a transformation that is unique among Dutch seventeenth-century painters.

Joseph distributing corn in Egypt

Only three dated paintings are documented in the seven years between Breenbergh's *Martyrdom of St Lawrence* of 1647 and the first of his two late canvases of *Joseph distributing corn in Egypt* of 1654.[17] Even allowing for a substantial number of losses, this suggests that the artist's rate of production decreased significantly during his later years. As always with Breenbergh, the reasons for this are impossible to ascertain. But one thing is clear: it cannot be due to a decline in his creative powers. On the contrary, it is widely acknowledged that the two versions of *Joseph in Egypt* that form the focus of the present exhibition reveal the master at the very summit of his art.

Since these two works are nearly identical, it is best to discuss their subject and style as though they were one. The source is Genesis XLI, 53-7. Sold into slavery in Egypt, Joseph has been appointed ruler of the country by Pharaoh and is in charge of storing up the harvest during seven good years to sell it to the Egyptians in the seven lean years that follow. Breenbergh portrays the hectic exchanges in the market-place that ensue. At the upper right is Joseph, regally clad and overseeing the proceedings, his erect and frontal pose signalling his authority. Seated on a balcony at the upper left is Pharaoh, who gazes on pensively. He is shielded by a parasol, as Joseph himself was in Breenbergh's version of

this subject in 1644. This seemingly modest alteration indicates that the artist has carefully rethought the subject; for the motif implies a pampered and protected position more appropriate to Pharaoh than to the 'upstart' Joseph.

The scene opens in the foreground left, with an elegantly clad woman tipping some coins into the hands of a barefooted youth, an action that epitomises the theme of the picture: the giving of charity. With this means, the beggar boy will be able to purchase a ration of corn. Surrounding them are a range of heads - both human and animal - of remarkable tenderness and individuality. In the foreground right, a muscular youth, viewed from behind, reclines on a sack of corn. He was last seen in the *St John the Baptist preaching* (fig. 7) of 1643 and, as in that picture, here seems to symbolise the humblest stratum of human existence, benefiting from

Fig. 13, Jacopo Pontormo, *Joseph in Egypt*, National Gallery, London

God's grace. Behind him, figures carry off their rations of corn, exchange money or possessions for it, or simply give thanks to the Lord. Particularly striking is the episode of a youth attempting to restrain a goat from eating some corn which he has spilled onto the ground. Far from being offered in exchange for the precious nourishment, the animal here helps itself to it! Above these figures, a group of tax gatherers, seated around a table, count their money or tally their accounts, while others carry additional sacks of corn from Joseph's store. The building from which they emerge is based on the basilica of Sta Maria in Aracoeli, Rome, which is approached by a large flight of steps. Contrasted with the obelisk at the left, which sets the scene in Egypt, it is probably also intended to serve a symbolic role. Since Joseph was seen as a prefiguration of Christ, the church here appears to stand for the new order which will supplant that of the Old Testament, represented by Pharaoh and the obelisk.

Even in the context of Breenbergh's mercurial development, the style of these pictures is remarkable, the foreground figures being among the largest he had ever attempted and the handling throughout of a fastidious precision. The draughtsmanship is exquisitely refined, the colouring immaculate in its purity and intensity, and the characterisation of individual figures and animals worthy of a born portraitist. This may be seen in the introspective gaze of a grey-haired man who forms part of the crowd nestled behind the woman and youth in the left foreground, or in the captivating glance of a blonde-haired youth who surveys the scene in the right middle distance, immediately behind two men struggling to support a sack of corn. In instances such as these, Breenbergh deserves to be regarded as the only important landscape painter of the seventeenth century to have successfully made the transition to figure painting in his later years, though other, even greater artists - such as Elsheimer, Rubens, Rembrandt and Nicolas Poussin - accomplished the reverse. In order to achieve this, however, Breenbergh resorted to a technique that was as idiosyncratic as his overall career progression: culling from isolated and unrelated sources until he could stitch together a composition worthy of his teeming imagination.

Though many of the motifs in the picture - such as the moneychangers, the semi-nude figures holding a basket of corn, or the soulful animals - derive from Lastman's canonical treatment of this subject (fig. 8) and also recur in Breenbergh's own version of the theme of 1644 (cat. 7), other features of the picture are strikingly new in the artist's career and have precedents far removed from the Pre-Rembrandtists. Among these are the

Fig. 14, Marten de Vos, *Joseph's Brethren preparing to depart from Egypt*, present whereabouts unknown

Fig. 15 (No. 2), Bartholomeus Breenbergh, *Joseph distributing corn in Egypt*, 1655, The Barber Institute of Fine Arts

centrifugal composition and the abrupt spatial elisions between planes, which result in startling juxtapositions between large and very small figures. Both of these features may be found in Pontormo's *Joseph in Egypt* (fig. 13) of c. 1515, which also contains the extensive flight of steps of Breenbergh's picture and, although not an upright canvas, is very nearly square and, in this respect, anticipates the more compressed format of Breenbergh's works of the 1650s. Since Pontormo's painting was probably in the Aldobrandini collection in Rome by 1603, Breenbergh might well have known the original, which also possesses the sheened brushwork and enamel-like surface colouring of his own works on this subject. Although a mannerist

Fig. 16, Guido Reni, *St Andrew led to his martyrdom*, 1608, Chapel of St Andrea, San Gregorio Magno, Rome

influence upon Breenbergh might seem surprising at this late stage of his career, it is merely another unexpected turn in his extraordinary development. Moreover, Pontormo's method of treating this theme had travelled north long before Breenbergh and was already familiar to such Flemish mannerists as Marten de Vos, whose *Joseph's Brethren preparing to depart from Egypt* (fig. 14) exhibits a comparably eccentric composition.[18]

As if all of these sources were not enough, Breenbergh borrowed even further when concocting this masterpiece. Also recalled from his years in Rome were the Pantheon, visible in the background centre, and the so-called Farnese Flora that adorns the staircase. This is a Roman copy of a Greek statue of Aphrodite that was in the Palazzo Farnese in Rome from the mid-sixteenth century onwards and is now in the Museo Nazionale, Naples. More surprising still is the source for the aristocratic young woman giving alms at the left of the picture, who is cribbed - down to the folds of her headdress and drapery! - from a young mother leading her child uphill to witness

St Andrew's martyrdom in Guido Reni's fresco of this theme of 1608 in San Gregorio Magno, Rome (fig. 16), which Breenbergh certainly knew, since a drawing of this church survives by him (cat. 21).

After this it may well be wondered if anything in Breenbergh's picture is original, and the answer is a great deal, not least its sheer artistic quality. The introduction of camels, the motifs of almsgiving and thanksgiving, and the penetratingly described bystanders - all of these are the artist's own. The last of them is among Breenbergh's chief innovations and one of the most engaging features of his art. In all other versions of this theme, virtually every figure is given something to do and the action appears carefully rehearsed and choreographed, like a scene from a play. But Breenbergh employs any number of supernumeraries who have no action at all to perform. Instead, they merely stand by and look on, lending the scene a candid and unpremeditated quality that could only have emanated from an artist who came to history painting via landscape and portraiture, seemingly ignorant of any of its 'rules'.

Fig. 17, Bartholomeus Breenbergh, *Alexander and Diogenes*, 1656, present whereabouts unknown

Breenbergh's undeniably idiosyncratic approach to this theme must have met with some favour. How else to explain the existence of an exact replica of the picture? - the only such instance of this known in the artist's career. Though Breenbergh had often repeated the same subjects throughout his life, never before had he repeated the identical picture. Nor can one imagine this to have been anything other than tedious for one with so fecund an imagination. While the circumstances that occasioned the second version will probably never be known, they can be surmised. Since it is dated one year after the first version, the Barber Institute replica was presumably commissioned by someone who coveted the 1654 painting but could not own it and, hence, requested Breenbergh to do as exact a copy of it as possible.

Comparing photographs of them, the only differences that emerge are in the pattern of trees and clouds in the background and in the inclusion of an additional margin of space in the foreground of the Birmingham version. But other variations may emerge in this, the first exhibition in which they have ever been seen together.

So far as we know, Breenbergh executed only one major history painting after the two versions of *Joseph distributing corn in Egypt*. This was an upright version of *Alexander and Diogenes* (fig. 17), signed and dated 1656 and no longer traceable.[19] Like the pictures that form the focus of the present exhibition, it depicts the main figures to either side of the composition and an elaborate cityscape beyond. This arrangement again evokes the art of the Italian mannerists, but the scale of the figures and the rhetorical nature of their gestures appear even more highly developed than those of its predecessors and confirm the fact that, by the last years of his career, Breenbergh had re-invented himself as a monumental history painter.

Its Later Influence

One of the greatest surprises awaiting any student of the chameleon-like Breenbergh is the discovery that this late developer as a history painter exerted a significant influence upon other artists. Given the undisputed quality of his works in this vein, this is anything but surprising. But given their very small numbers and Breenbergh's close association with landscape painting, one might have expected them to go largely unnoticed by his contemporaries. Yet nothing could be further from the truth. Though the groundwork for this may have been laid by the handful of reproductive engravings by Breenbergh and others made after certain of his most ambitious history paintings - most notably the 1644 *Joseph in Egypt* and the *Martyrdom of St Lawrence* - the late canvases of *Joseph in Egypt* also exerted considerable influence upon his contemporaries; and these were not engraved at all.

Johannes Lingelbach's *View of the Forum Romanum* (cat. 10) of 1656 is the first work that reveals the deep impression made by Breenbergh's composition. Set in a Roman market-place, whose architectural composition is closely comparable to that of Breenbergh's picture, this depicts a seventeenth-century scene of buying, selling, barter and buffoonery that forms a light-hearted complement to the urgency and desperation of Breenbergh's picture. Though Lingelbach's caricatural figures are no match for the tenderness and humanity of those of his model, and the scale of his figures is considerably smaller, it is conceivable that the relationship between the two works may be even closer than this.

Lingelbach's canvas is signed and dated at the left - exactly as Breenbergh's two works - and is virtually identical to them in size. Given that it was executed only one year after the second *Joseph in Egypt*, is it conceivable that it was intended as a pendant to one of Breenbergh's pictures on this subject? As ever with this mysterious artist, we will almost certainly never know. But it is not difficult to imagine a scenario in which this might have been so. Let us suppose that the recipient of either of Breenbergh's canvases decided to provide it with a pendant. The artist may have been approached to execute this and refused on any number of grounds: he was nearing the end of his career, he had rarely conceived of works as pairs, etc. Thus, his patron was forced to turn elsewhere - to an artist of the younger generation, recently returned from Italy, who could supply him with a seventeenth-century Roman market scene to complement his Old Testament one by Breenbergh.

In the same year as Lingelbach completed his contemporary counterpart to Breenbergh's masterpiece, the history painter Nicolaes de Helt Stockade (1614-69) executed an overmantel of *Joseph distributing corn in Egypt* (fig. 18) for the Treasury Ordinary in the newly completed Amsterdam Town Hall.[20] Commissioned for the room allocated to those responsible for managing the city's finances and supervising public works, the picture was considered appropriate for this setting, as one of the roles of the treasurers was to buy up surplus grain and sell it to residents at reasonable prices during shortages. Priding themselves on their charity and compassion, the Dutch often commissioned works of art that reflected these qualities, among them numerous depictions of Joseph in Egypt, which may explain Breenbergh's repeated attachment to this theme.[21] How galling it must have been for him, then, to witness a minor painter of the younger generation landing such a plum commission, especially when the work that resulted was so manifestly indebted to his own!

Helt Stockade's inspiration was not Breenbergh's two

Fig. 18, Nicolaes de Helt Stockade, *Joseph distributing corn in Egypt*, 1656, Royal Palace, Amsterdam

canvases of this theme of the mid-1650s, though the presence of an obelisk and the Pantheon in the background suggests that these were already familiar to him. Rather it was from the 1644 version of the subject that he derived most of his invention, including the parasol over Joseph, the distraught mother surrendering her children to him, the moneychangers with their accompanying still life and the nude man with the sack of corn at the lower right. Where he differs from Breenbergh, however, is in the crowding of his figures and the somewhat histrionic nature of their gestures. In contrast, the measured intervals and restrained poses of Breenbergh's picture possess a clarity and articulacy that combine the narrative inventiveness of Lastman with the epic grandeur of Raphael and his school.

Thirteen years after Helt Stockade executed his picture, Rembrandt's pupil of the late 1630s, Ferdinand Bol (1616-80), painted a *Joseph in Egypt* (cat. 11) for the Nieuwe Kerk in Amsterdam. An earlier version of the composition, in reverse, was also made by the artist as part of a set of mural decorations for a house in Utrecht, probably in the mid-1650s.[22] Both of these relate to Helt Stockade's canvas in the imperious figure of Joseph, seen in profile and commanding the Egyptians to exchange their most precious possessions for sacks of grain. The architectural setting and florid figure style of the picture likewise link him with this work. But, by whatever means, Bol had also caught sight of Breenbergh's composition of this subject of the mid-1650s by the time he tackled his own; and several motifs stuck in his mind. Among them were the man with the bulging brow bearing away his ration of corn and the man bearing a sack of grain over his head at the upper right of the picture. Given Bol's adherence to the bland and classicising style of much Dutch history painting of this period, such motifs may seem no more than idiosyncratic details lost in the general tumult of the whole. But they do confirm what Breenbergh himself probably had little cause to expect: namely, that his thoughts on treating this subject would exert an indelible impression upon his colleagues, even if none of them would rival his idiosyncratic - and wholly engaging - approach to the theme.[23]

In retrospect, Breenbergh's two compositions of *Joseph distributing corn in Egypt* are arguably the finest produced by any Dutch master of the period. That of 1644 possesses a remarkable clarity and cohesion, even when appraised through mere copies and prints. And the two versions of the mid-1650s boast an originality and inexhaustible inventiveness that qualify the artist to be considered among the great narrative painters of his day. To be sure, they are eccentric, elliptical and 'impure', with their wealth of animals and onlookers, their helter-skelter activity and abrupt changes of scale. In the end, however, it is such quirks as these that make them so memorable when compared with the more orthodox creations of Breenbergh's contemporaries. A master of the bizarre and fantastic from the very beginning of his career, the artist here crowns his achievement with works brimming with vitality and a kaleidoscopic range of actors and incidents conceived as though in a dream - or by a stream of consciousness.

[1] The documents concerning Breenbergh's life have been fully published by Door H. J. Nalis, 'Bartholomeus Breenbergh, Aantekeningen over zijn leven en verwanten', *Vereeniging tot beofening van Overijsselsch...*, Kampen, 1972, pp. 62-81 and 'Bartholomeus Breenbergh, Aanvullende gegevens betreffende zijn ouders', *Vereeniging tot beofening van Overijsselsch...*, Zwolle, 1973, pp. 51- 9.

[2] R1981, pp. 4 and 25; Werner Sumowski, *Gemälde der Rembrandt Schüler*, I, Landau/Pfalz, 1983, p. 202, nos. 68-9.

[3] A. Dézaillier d'Argenville, *Abrégé de la vie des plus fameux peintres...*, III, Paris, 1762, pp. 149.

[4] R1981, p. 41, no. 64; *The Hallwyl Collection of Paintings*, Hallwylska Museet, Stockholm, 1997, p. 135, no. 58.

[5] Quoted in Astrid Tümpel and Peter Schatborn, *Pieter Lastman, the man who taught Rembrandt*, Rembrandthuis, Amsterdam, 1991, p. 16.

[6] F. W. H. Hollstein, *Dutch and Flemish Etchings, Engravings and Woodcuts, ca. 1450-1700*, III, Amsterdam, 1950, p. 207.

[7] R1981, pp. 54-5, no. 116; 56, no. 123; and 58-9, no. 133.

[8] Tümpel and Schatborn, *op. cit.*, pp. 74-7.

[9] R1981, pp. 72-3, nos. 177-80.

[10] *Ibid.*, pp. 79-80, nos. 202-202a.

[11] Michael North, *Art and Commerce in the Dutch Golden Age*, New Haven and London, 1997, pp. 99-100.

[12] National Gallery of Art, Washington, D.C., and elsewhere, *Gods, Saints and Heroes, Dutch Painting in the Art of Rembrandt*, 1980, pp. 65-76.

[13] For which, see especially Tümpel and Schatborn, *op. cit.*, pp. 30-2.

[14] Cf. Astrid Tümpel, 'Claes Cornelisz. Moeyaert', *Oud Holland*, Vol. 88, 1974, pp. 93-6, 115-7, and 121-3 (for a later version of the theme of c. 1650).

[15] Cf. Musée des Beaux-Arts, Lyon. Cf. Jacques Foucart, 'Le sacrifice d'Elie au Mont Carmel par Barthomeus (*sic*) Breenbergh', *Bulletin des musées et monuments lyonnais*, no. 3-4, 1991, pp. 42-55.

[16] R1981, pp. 84-5, no. 213.

[17] *Adoration of the Magi* (1648), sold Sotheby's (with P. de Boer, Amsterdam, 1985); *Capriccio with Roman Ruins* (1650), R1991, pp. 62-5; *Antique Sacrifice* (1651), R1981, p. 92, no. 240.

[18] Sold Christie's, London. 14. 5. 1965, lot 118.

[19] R1981, pp. 90-1, no. 235.

[20] For which, see especially Sjoerd Faber, *Van heren, die hun stoel en kussen niet beschaemen (Of lords, who seat nor cushion do ashame: the government of Amsterdam in the 17th and 18th centuries)*, Royal Palace, Amsterdam, 1987, pp. 36-8.

[21] Christian Tümpel and others, *Im Lichte Rembrandts, Das Alte Testament im Goldenen Zeitalter der niederländischen Kunst*, Westfälisches Museum, Münster, 1994, pp. 44-5.

[22] Albert Blankert, *Ferdinand Bol (1616-1680)*, Doornspijk, 1982, p. 95, nos. 12 and 13.

[23] For yet another of many treatments of the theme that appears to depend upon an amalgam of sources from Lastman to Breenbergh, see Gerbrand van den Eeckhout's drawing of c. 1664-6 (Louvre, Paris; cf. Werner Sumowski, *Drawings of the Rembrandt School*, New York, 1977, III, p. 1432).

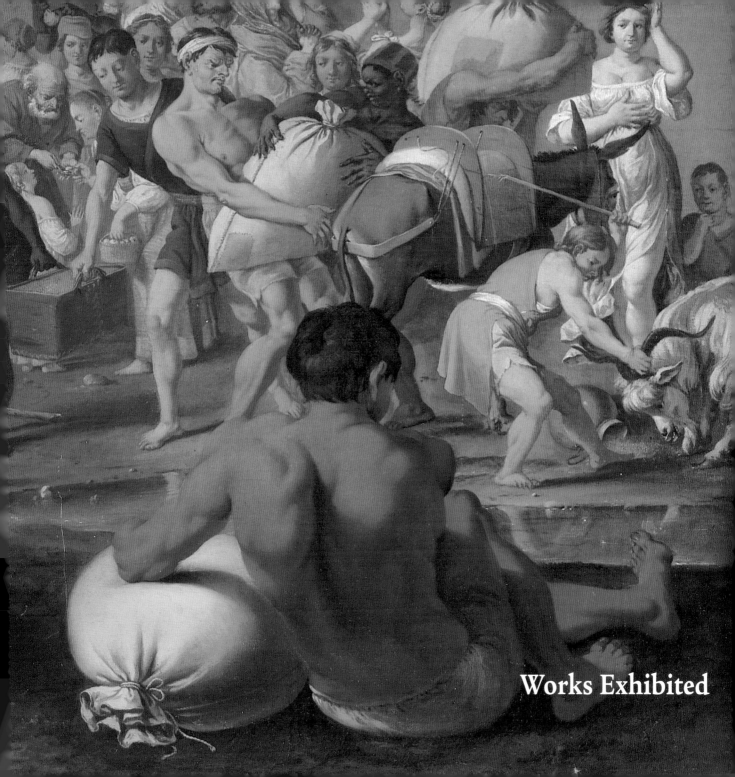

Works Exhibited

Paintings

Bartholomeus Breenbergh (1598 - 1657)

1 *Joseph distributing corn in Egypt,* 1654
Inscribed lower left: Barts Breenbergh fecit/A° 1654
Oil on canvas, 111.8 x 88.9 cm.
Private Collection, United Kingdom

The subject is from Genesis XLI, 53-59. Joseph has been sold into slavery in Egypt by his brothers and imprisoned by Pharaoh for allegedly raping Potiphar's wife. He redeems himself as an interpreter of Pharaoh's dreams, warning his master that the kingdom faces seven good harvests followed by seven years of famine. In return, Pharaoh frees him from prison and appoints him leader of the Egyptians, storing corn during the good years so that he might be able to sell it during those of hardship. Though the Bible does not stipulate what the people exchange for this precious nourishment, artists typically portray it as livestock, money or jewellery.

The most complex and ambitious of Breenbergh's upright history paintings, this picture depicts Joseph at the upper right, overseeing the distribution of the grain, and Pharaoh, seated, at the upper left, shielded by a parasol and flanked by an obelisk, symbol of the old order, which Joseph is superseding. To the right of it is the Pantheon. The building at the extreme right, reached by a long flight of steps, is based on the church of Sta Maria in Aracoeli, Rome, which once marked the site of a market-place. In the foreground, figures barter for corn while, immediately below Joseph, a group of moneychangers, seated around a table, tally the accounts of the sale.

The picture is the subject of the only known replica to survive by Breenbergh (cat. 2), who had earlier treated the theme in a lost canvas (cat. 7) that was to prove the most influential work of his entire career. Whereas the latter owes its greatest debt to the art of the Pre-Rembrandtists - especially Lastman (fig. 8) - the present work is a surprising throwback in its dependence instead upon such Italian mannerist masters as Pontormo (fig. 13), from whom Breenbergh derived the somewhat elliptical design, in which the main incidents are relegated to the extremities of the picture. The striking figure of a turbaned and richly clad young woman at the left derives from Guido Reni's fresco of *St Andrew led to Martyrdom* (fig. 16) of 1608 in the church of San Gregorio Magno, Rome, which Breenbergh almost certainly knew, as he made a drawing of this church (cat. 21).

The painting is first recorded in the collection of the Marquis of Bute in 1800 and was much admired by Sir Ellis Waterhouse when he visited Mount Stuart on 25 July 1949 and noted that it was 'very unusual and in excellent condition'.[1] This may well have prompted him, in 1963, to purchase the replica of the work for the Barber Institute, where he was director between 1952 and 1970.

For a fuller account of the picture's place in Breenbergh's career, see the introductory essay, pp. 23-7.

1 Quoted in National Gallery of Scotland, Edinburgh, *Dutch Art and Scotland*, by Julia Lloyd-Williams, 1992, p. 70.

References: R1981, pp. 289-90, no. 230; R1991, pp. 66-9, no. 26; National Gallery of Scotland, Edinburgh, *Dutch Art and Scotland*, by Julia Lloyd-Williams, 1992, p. 70, no. 11; Dulwich Picture Gallery, *Inspired by Italy, Dutch Landscape Painting 1600 - 1700*, by Laurie B. Harwood, 2002, p. 92, no. 11.

Fig. 19 (No. 1), Bartholomeus Breenbergh, *Joseph distributing corn in Egypt*, 1654,
Private Collection, United Kingdom

2   *Joseph distributing corn in Egypt,* 1655
   Inscribed lower left: Bart^s Breenbergh fecit/An° 1655
   Oil on canvas, 110.5 x 90 cm.
   The Barber Institute of Fine Arts,
   The University of Birmingham
   (reproduced on page 25)

The only surviving replica by the artist, this picture's subject and significance in Breenbergh's career are fully discussed in the entry for its prototype (cat. 1) and in the introductory essay to the catalogue, pp. 23-7.

The Barber Institute's painting was once in the collection of the Counts Czernin, which also boasted Vermeer's sublime *Artist in his Studio* (Kunsthistorisches Museum, Vienna). Dated one year after the original canvas, it differs from it primarily in the pattern of clouds across the sky and the foliage of the trees, though other differences may emerge in this first-ever confrontation between the two works. One feature that does distinguish them is the brilliance of colouring and tonality of the present picture, compared with the more muted appearance of the version of 1654. This is likely to be the result of differences in condition.

Although Breenbergh had treated the subject in the previous decade (cat. 7), in the manner of the Pre-Rembrandtists, his two canvases of the 1650s are among his most original - and eccentric - history paintings in their eclectic range of sources, which include works by Italian Renaissance and seventeenth-century masters (fig. 13 & 16) in addition to those of Lastman (fig. 8) and his followers. Together with the artist's earlier version of this subject, these works exerted a profound influence upon the art of his contemporaries and followers. Johannes Lingelbach, Ferdinand Bol and others (cat. 10 & 11; & fig. 18) reflected an awareness of one or both of Breenbergh's versions of this theme, elevating him to a position of unexpected prominence among Dutch history painters given that he had devoted most of his career to landscape.

As is the case with the vast majority of Breenbergh's pictures, no drawings survive for this painting or its prototype, the creative evolution of the artist's works being one of the greatest of the many mysteries that surround his career.

References: R1981, p. 90, no. 231; Westfälisches Landesmuseum, Münster, *Im Lichte Rembrandts, Das Alte Testament im Goldenen Zeitalter der niederländischen Kunst*, 1994, p. 253, no. 26.

3   *Landscape with Mercury and Argus,* c. 1630
   Oil on copper, 30.5 x 49.5 cm.
   Private Collection, Europe

Painted on copper, a support much favoured by Elsheimer (fig. 4), this idyllic landscape marks a transition between the works of Breenbergh's Italian years and those of his return to the Netherlands and is datable to c. 1630. Though its lush and verdant scenery is decidedly northern in character, the ruins in the background - which Roethlisberger has identified as those of the Temple of Venus and Roma on the Roman Forum[1] - testify to the artist's sojourn in Italy.

The subject is from Ovid, *Metamorphoses*, I, 675ff. Mercury has been sent by Juno to rescue Io, transformed into a heifer, from the care of the hundred-eyed monster Argus, who is guarding her with his flock. Removing his cap and wings, so that he resembles a shepherd, Mercury lulls Argus to sleep by serenading him. When the latter succumbs, Mercury will slay him and rescue the hapless Io, who appears at the far right. Breenbergh depicts the suspenseful moment when Mercury is seducing Argus with his song and separates them by a division in the landscape that signals their contending positions.

With its gnarled tree trunks, richly diversified foliage and irregular patterns of growth, the picture testifies to a

Fig. 20 (No. 3), Bartholomeus Breenbergh, *Landscape with Mercury and Argus*, Private Collection, Europe

new-found naturalism in Breenbergh's art. Underpinning this, however, is a firmly structured composition, in which clear framing elements to either side of the design open out to reveal a central vista, as in comparable works by the pioneer of the classical landscape tradition in Italy, Annibale Carracci (1560-1609).

The theme of Mercury and Argus was a popular one with seventeenth-century artists, inspiring major paintings by Rubens, Velázquez and Claude. All of these depict a far more confrontational encounter between the protagonists than does Breenbergh, whose isolated figures - with their pensive and undemonstrative poses - appear suspended, as though in a dream.

1   R1981, p. 55, no. 119.

Reference: see note above.

4 *Christ and the Nobleman of Capernaum,* c. 1631-4
Oil on panel, 37 x 51 cm.
Rafael Valls Ltd., London and
Hoogsteder & Hoogsteder, The Hague

Recently cleaned, this picture is a masterpiece of Breenbergh's career and a key work in his transition from landscape to history painting. Its subject is from Matthew, VIII, 5-13 and Luke VII, 1-10. Both gospels describe the encounter at Capernaum between Christ and a devout Roman centurion whose manservant is paralysed and confined to bed. In return for the centurion's faith, Christ heals the servant - the first of the miracles that he performs from a distance, without touching or seeing the recipient.

Breenbergh portrays the nobleman kneeling before Christ in a dignified yet supplicant pose which, greatly enlarged, would be worthy of Rubens. Surrounding them is a group of Roman soldiers and a cross-section of 'ordinary' humanity who react with wonderment and incredulity at the nobleman's faith. As Christ turns to the group on his left, signalling his intentions, a bent old woman, leaning on her stick, marvels at the centurion's confession, while his soldiers express their astonishment at his dedication to the Lord.

The picture is notable for its rich chromaticism, the resplendent lemon-yellow robes of the centurion forming the focus of the central group which is dramatically highlighted by a pool of light that embraces the action and separates it from the more delicate and silvery tones of the background. Particularly remarkable are the glistening accents of light on the soldiers' armour and helmets, the weathered surface of the temple at the right, and the meticulous rendering of the vegetation in the foreground, all of which reveal an artist highly sensitized to the subtleties of nature - and vision.

According to Roethlisberger, the building on the right is the Temple of Antoninus and Faustina on the Forum.[1]

The obelisk is a favourite device of Breenbergh's, which also occurs in his late versions of *Joseph distributing corn in Egypt.* It is presumably introduced here to symbolise the old order, rejected by the centurion, who chooses instead to follow the teachings of Christ.

Breenbergh may have been drawn to this subject by two versions of the theme by Moeyaert of 1629 and 1632, neither of which includes so elaborate a landscape nor so varied and expressive a group of figures.[2] He returned to the theme in 1637 in a panel (Kunsthalle, Karlsruhe), in which his familiar, diminutive figures enact the drama before a more spectacular landscape of antique ruins, buildings and mountains.[3]

The picture was much celebrated in the latter part of the eighteenth century, when it was in French collections, notably that of M. Poullain, Receveur Général des Domaines du Roi, whose posthumous sale catalogue included an engraving of the composition, in reverse, noting that it was one of Breenbergh's most precious works.[4]

Technical examination of the picture reveals that there were originally a standing man and two smaller figures behind him at the far left and that, although there is no underdrawing beneath any of the figures, it is visible in the temple at the right, which was extensively revised in the course of painting.

1 R1981, pp. 62-3, no. 146 (mistakenly identified as the Temple of Angustus and Faustina).
2 Astrid Tümpel, 'Claes Cornelisz. Moeyaert', *Oud Holland,* Vol. 88, 1974, pp. 88-92 and fig. 122 and 125.
3 R1981, p. 75, no. 187.
4 *Collection de cent-vingt estampes gravées d'après les tableaux et dessins qui composoient le cabinet de M. Poullain,* Paris, 1781, no. 19.

References: R1981, pp. 62-3, no. 146; R1991, p. 26, no. 9.

Fig. 21 (No. 4), Bartholomeus Breenbergh, *Christ and the Nobleman of Capernaum*,
Rafael Valls Ltd., London and Hoogsteder and Hoogsteder, The Hague

5 *Coastal Landscape with Saul after the Conversion*, 1633
Inscribed lower left: BBreenborch fecit/Aº.1633
Oil on canvas, 62 x 138 cm.
Rafael Valls Ltd., London and
Douwes Fine Art, Amsterdam

In Acts IX, 8-9, the Bible recounts the story of Saul on his way to Damascus to persecute the Christians, when he is suddenly blinded by a vision of the Lord. 'And Saul arose from the earth: and when his eyes were opened, he saw no man: but they led him by the hand, and brought him to Damascus. And he was three days without sight, and neither did eat nor drink.' Once arrived at Damascus, Saul was baptised as a Christian and, as St Paul, won countless converts to the faith.

This expansive landscape is Breenbergh's only treatment of this theme and derives its principal group from an engraving by Lucas van Leyden of 1509 from which the artist also borrowed the motif of a large rock behind the figures.[1] But, whereas the former depicts Saul in a submissive pose, his head hung low and his hands held by his companions, Breenbergh portrays him in a much more commanding stance, his head raised and arms extended, as though eagerly awaiting his forthcoming baptism and conversion.

The landscape is divided into two halves, the left hand side containing the dynamic figure group surrounded by precipitous terrain, as though to symbolise the dark and threatening forces that marked the start of Saul's journey. Primary colours accent the principal figures, with Saul

himself dressed in blue and red; while earthier tones describe his entourage, which includes soldiers on horseback, others bearing weapons and (at the left) the figure of a young mother attempting to console her weeping child. Leading directly to the main figure group - like an upbeat in music - is a carefree youth, balanced on one leg, who urges his bridled horse forward.

In the background right, appears the city of Damascus, bathed in a silvery light, its ethereal appearance contrasted strikingly with the more mundane landscape behind Saul. Through this division alone Breenbergh traces the protagonist's spiritual journey from ignorance to enlightenment, or darkness to light.

The elongated format of the picture, which permits the artist to depict a panoramic landscape, may indicate that the work was specially commissioned, perhaps for a particular setting over a window or door.

1 Jan Piet Filedt Kok, *The New Hollstein Dutch and Flemish Etchings, Engravings and Woodcuts 1450-1700*, Lucas van Leyden, Rotterdam, 1996, p. 113, no. 107.

References: R1981, p. 65, no. 154; The Montreal Museum of Fine Arts, *Italian Recollections, Dutch Painters of the Golden Age*, by Frederik J. Duparc and Linda L. Graif, 1990, pp. 96-7, no. 22; R1991, p. 28, no. 10; Dulwich Picture Gallery, London *Inspired by Italy, Dutch Landscape Painting 1600 - 1700*, by Laurie B. Harwood, 2002, p. 88, no. 9.

Fig. 22 (No. 5), Bartholomeus Breenbergh, *Coastal Landscape with Saul after the Conversion*, 1633, Rafael Valls Ltd., London and Douwes Fine Art, Amsterdam

6 *Landscape with the Finding of Moses,* 1636
Inscribed lower right: BBreenbergh.f./ A° 1636
Oil on panel, 41.5 x 56.7 cm.
The National Gallery, London

The Finding of Moses is the subject of Breenbergh's earliest dated painting (fig. 3) and became a firm favourite with the artist, who may have painted it as many as five times.[1] As an important historical subject that necessitated a landscape background, it enjoyed great popularity with artists adept at both of these, among them Veronese and Poussin.

The theme derives from Exodus II, 1-6. The infant Moses has been exposed on the waters by his mother, in accordance with an edict by Pharaoh. He is discovered by Pharaoh's daughter and her maidservants, who find him floating in a basket and, rescuing him, instruct an elderly woman - who turns out to be the child's true mother - to take him away and nurse him.

In this version, Pharaoh's daughter is shown instructing Moses's mother to tend the child while her companions look on. Particularly endearing is the unprepossessing appearance of the infant, who is wrapped in swaddling clothes, and the obeisance with which the old woman takes her orders from the imperiously profiled figure of Pharaoh's daughter. Behind them is a rich and diversified landscape divided by a river to either side of which are ancient buildings and remains. Framing the principal figure group from above are an obelisk and a pyramid. Together with the camels and elephant in the distance, these serve to set the scene in Egypt. According to Roethlisberger, the stele on the left is based on Giacomo della Porta's fountain in the Roman Forum.[2]

The picture is remarkable for its delicate, pearly colouring, the distant vista being woven out of the subtlest range of blues, greys, greens and creams. Along with the rhythmically integrated relationship between the figure group and the surrounding landscape, this makes it arguably the most successful of all the artist's treatments of this familiar subject.

Like many others of Breenbergh's finest works, the *Finding of Moses* was in a French collection in the eighteenth and early-nineteenth centuries. It was left to the National Gallery as part of the Richard Simmons bequest in 1847, and remains the only work by the artist in the collection.

1 R1981, pp. 41, no. 64; 69, no. 168; 73-4, no. 182 (the present picture); 78, no. 196 and Montreal Museum of Fine Arts, *Italian Recollections, Dutch Painters of the Golden Age*, by Frederik J. Duparc and Linda L. Graif, 1990, pp. 100-1, no. 24.
2 R1981, pp. 73-4, no. 182.

References: R1981, pp. 73-4, no. 182; Neil MacLaren, *Catalogue of the Dutch School 1600-1900*, revised and expanded by Christopher Brown, National Gallery, London, 1991, pp. 55-6; Dulwich Picture Gallery, London, *Inspired by Italy, Dutch Landscape Painting 1600-1700*, by Laurie B. Harwood, 2002, p. 90, no. 10.

Fig. 23 (No. 6), Bartholomeus Breenbergh, *Landscape with the Finding of Moses*, 1636, The National Gallery, London

7 *Joseph distributing corn in Egypt* (after Breenbergh), attributed to Jan de Bisschop (1628-71)
Oil on canvas, 105 x 130 cm.
Belasting & Douane Museum, Rotterdam,
The Netherlands

Judging by the number of copies and variants made after it, this was by far the most influential and widely imitated work of Breenbergh's career.[1] Many of these derivatives may, admittedly, have been based on the two etchings of the composition by the artist himself (cat. 23) and by his pupil Jan de Bisschop (cat. 24). But the very existence of the prints attests to the design's widespread popularity during Breenbergh's lifetime; and, in retrospect, both the painted copies and etchings have served to fill a vital gap in our knowledge of the artist. For Breenbergh's original panel of this theme was destroyed by bombing in Dresden in 1945, and not even a photograph of it exists. It is represented here by a fine painted copy attributed to his close follower, Jan de Bisschop, which is approximately twice the size of the original picture.

The subject is the same as that of the versions of this theme of the mid-1650s (cat. 1-2) and shows Joseph, shielded by a parasol, distributing corn to the famine-stricken Egyptians, who exchange money, livestock or jewellery for it. In the centre left, moneychangers, seated around a table, tally their accounts, and, to the right of them, a mother with her three children and her own aged mother implores Joseph to accept a precious necklace in exchange for grain. As her eldest child wipes the tears from its eyes, two infants languish at her knees. Taken together, this figure group represents the three ages of man - all ultimately dependent upon Joseph's charity and compassion.

The composition is heavily indebted to Lastman's pioneering treatment of the theme of 1612 (fig. 8), which also influenced four later versions of the subject by Jan Pynas (1618) and Claes Cornelisz Moeyaert (1633, 1644 and c. 1650), one of the latter-day Pre-Rembrandtists with whom Breenbergh was most closely associated (fig. 9).[2] But whereas all of these works depict the figures huddled together in a single mass, Breenbergh gives his work a more lucid and highly articulated structure, with gaps - or breathing spaces - surrounding the individual figure groups. These enable one to 'read' the composition more easily and to contemplate the contribution of each individual episode to the whole. The greater clarity and legibility of this approach far exceed anything achieved by Lastman or his followers and reveal Breenbergh's superior gifts both as a narrative painter and designer - features that call to mind the monumental history paintings on comparable themes by his Italian predecessors and contemporaries (fig. 10).

The picture differs from Breenbergh's two later versions of the subject in its landscape format - which conforms with that of Lastman and his followers - and in its more straightforward treatment of the narrative, which enlists all of the participants to contribute to the story in an active and purposeful manner. In this respect, it may be seen as among the artist's most Lastman-like creations, the two later versions introducing a tone of fantasy and eccentricity that bears little in common with the Pre-Rembrandtists. This may also explain why the present picture was Breenbergh's most celebrated work, for it reveals him as a master of a rational and classical style of history painting which could be readily imitated, unlike the more personal and idiosyncratic versions of the 1650s.

1 The photographic archive of the Rijksbureau voor Kunsthistorische Documentatie in The Hague contains photographs of at least nine copies (or partial copies) of the picture.
2 Cf. Kurt Bauch, 'Beiträge zum Werk der Vorläufer Rembrandts, I. Die Gemälde des Jan Pynas', *Oud Holland*, LII, 1935, p. 154 and fig. 11 and Astrid Tümpel and Peter Schatborn, *Pieter Lastman, the man who taught Rembrandt*, Rembrandthuis, Amsterdam, 1991, p. 30 and fig. 18 (for Pynas); Astrid Tümpel, 'Claes Cornelisz. Moeyaert', *Oud Holland*, Vol. 88, 1974, pp. 93-5, fig. 126; 115-17, fig. 154-6 and 121-3, fig. 167.

Reference: R1981, pp. 80-2, no. 204.

Fig. 24 (No. 7), Attributed to Jan de Bisschop (after Breenbergh), *Joseph distributing corn in Egypt*, Belasting & Douane Museum, Rotterdam, The Netherlands

8 *Amaryllis crowning Mirtillo,* c. 1645
Inscribed lower left: B. Breenbergh fecit.
Oil on canvas, 77 x 101 cm.
The Bowes Museum, Barnard Castle, Co. Durham

This is one of Breenbergh's rare depictions of a subject from the literature of his own day and takes its theme from Giovanni Battista Guarini's pastoral drama, *Il pastor fido* ('The Faithful Shepherd'), first published in 1590, which enjoyed great popularity not only in Italy but in France, Flanders, and the Netherlands, van Dyck being the greatest painter of the theme.

The scene is set in Arcadia, where an oracle has decreed that the land would be visited by plagues until two of its inhabitants - a faithless nymph and a faithful shepherd - were united. In Act II, Scene I of this work, the amorous nymph Amaryllis organises a kissing contest among her nymphs, whereupon the faithful shepherd Mirtillo, who is in love with her, disguises himself as a woman and wins the contest. Amaryllis crowns him and the couple are eventually united, sparing Arcadia the ravages of the plague.

Breenbergh depicts the crowning ceremony that concludes this contest, showing Mirtillo kneeling before Amaryllis while her nymphs gaze on. In the right hand corner two of them continue to engage in a kissing spree oblivious to the fact that the competition has already been won. Behind the figures is an imposing landscape of classical buildings and remains that opens out in the centre to a distant vista. The device of positioning the key figures to either side of the picture, with a gap between them, is a recurring one in the art of Breenbergh, who evidently delighted in such centrifugal compositions, which may also be seen in his late versions of *Joseph distributing corn in Egypt.*

The picture probably dates from c. 1645 and is consistent with works of this period in its comparatively large-scale figures and in their prominent positioning in the foreground plane. Both of these features testify to the artist's increasing interest in history painting from the mid-1640s - one which is evident here in the fact that, although the disposition of the landscape is a familiar one with Breenbergh, the figure group is entirely new.

Reference: R1981, p. 84, no. 212.

Fig. 25 (No. 8), Bartholomeus Breenbergh, *Amaryllis crowning Mirtillo*, The Bowes Museum, Barnard Castle, Co. Durham

9 *The Martyrdom of St Lawrence,* 1647
Inscribed lower right: BBreenbergh f A° 1647
Oil on canvas, 86.8 x 102 cm.
Städelsches Kunstinstitut, Frankfurt am Main

The most populous - and tumultuous - of all of the artist's history paintings, this picture takes its subject from the Golden Legend, I, 736-55. St Lawrence, a deacon of the church under Pope Sixtus II, was martyred in Rome in 258 for refusing to adhere to the pagan faith and was put to death by being roasted on a gridiron.

Breenbergh depicts the climax of the action, with the saint lying on the grill as the Roman soldiers stoke the flames. At the right three pagan priests castigate him for his beliefs, one of them pointing vehemently at a statue of Mercury holding his caduceus and a moneybag, an attribute of his role as the patron of commerce. In the distance, Roman soldiers - some of them on horseback - restrain the crowds eager to witness the execution; and, riding in at the left is the Emperor Valerian, commanding the proceedings.

The background includes a number of important Roman landmarks. On the left is the Column of Trajan and, in the distance, the Castel Sant'Angelo and St Peter's. The building at the right has been identified by Roethlisberger as the temple of Antonius and Faustina which, according to him, became one of the buildings dedicated to St Lawrence.[1] The statue of Mercury is based on Michelangelo's *Bacchus* of c. 1496-8 (Bargello, Florence).

The picture has one of the most complex ancestries of any of Breenbergh's works. Its starting-point was almost certainly the visionary treatments of the theme by Titian, which the artist must at least have known from Cort's engraving of 1571 (cat. 26). From this he would have derived the motifs of the recumbent saint on the grill, the statue of an antique deity at the upper right, the soldier prodding the saint and the kneeling man, seen from behind, in the foreground right. Whereas Titian's figure stokes the flames, however, that by Breenbergh holds a basket of wood, as in Rubens's altarpiece of this theme of

c. 1615 (Alte Pinakothek, Munich).

The subject had also been painted by Poelenburgh in 1622-4 (Staatliche Kunstsammlungen, Kassel) in the landscape format adopted by Breenbergh.[2] Far more obscure than these sources, however, is that of the antique, which probably accounts for the figure of the kneeling youth at the centre left, who blows on the hot flames. He bears an uncanny similarity to a legendary achievement of the Greek painter, Antiphilus, of the 4th century BC, who (according to Pliny) won praise 'for his figure of a boy blowing a fire, and for the reflection cast... on the boy's face'.[3]

Though the composition possesses a strong central axis, the preponderance of buildings and figures to either side of the canvas is increasingly characteristic of the artist and reaches its most extreme expression in the two late versions of *Joseph distributing corn in Egypt*. It was perhaps in an attempt to rein in the potential discursiveness of this arrangement that Breenbergh adopted the more concentrated, upright format for his later history pictures.

Even to the naked eye it is evident that there are prominent *pentimenti* in the putto in the sky, descending with the martyr's palm, and in the banner to the right of it. The architectural background, too, shows clear signs of having been built up by painting the foreground buildings over those behind them.

The composition was justly celebrated in a masterful etching by Breenbergh's follower, Jan de Bisschop (cat. 25), and the original canvas has a distinguished provenance, having been in the collection of the court painter to Louis XV, Jacques André J C Aved (1702-66), in the mid-eighteenth century.

1 R1981, p. 89, no. 228.

2 Another *Martyrdom of St Lawrence*, attributed to Breenbergh and much closer in design to Poelenburgh's picture, was sold at Christie's, London, 10 July 1992, lot 153.

3 *Historia Naturalis*, XXXV, 138.

References: R1981, p. 89, no. 228; Städelsches Kunstinstitut, Frankfurt am Main, *Niederländische Gemälde vor 1800 im Städel*, by Jochen Sander and Bodo Brinkmann, Frankfurt am Main, 1995, p. 22.

Fig. 26 (No. 9), Bartholomeus Breenbergh, *The Martyrdom of St Lawrence*, 1647, Städelsches Kunstinstitut, Frankfurt am Main

Related Artists

10 ***View of the Forum Romanum,*** 1656,
    by Johannes Lingelbach (1622-74)
    Inscribed centre left: Lingelbach/fecit/1656
    Oil on canvas, 115 x 89.5 cm.
    Private Collection, Europe

This is the earliest work to reflect an awareness of Breenbergh's two versions of *Joseph distributing corn in Egypt* of 1654-5 and dates from a year after the Barber Institute picture. Since it is virtually identical in size to both of them, and shares a common horizon line, it is possible - though, alas, unprovable - that it was commissioned as a pendant to one of these pictures, the Breenbergh depicting an Old Testament market scene set in Egypt and that by Lingelbach a contemporary one set in Rome.

The painting depicts a welter of figures trading, begging, bartering or merely socialising in the Roman Forum and takes the form of a light-hearted complement to Breenbergh's more earnest composition. Particularly diverting is the motif of a monkey performing for the crowd at the right and the witty contrasts between the grandiloquence of the buildings and statuary and the lowly demeanour of the human inhabitants of the scene.

The setting is a kind of Roman *capriccio* which is, on the one hand, surprisingly literal but, in the end, utterly fanciful. The building at the extreme right is the back of Santa Maria Antigua, which was rebuilt early in the eighteenth century and renamed Santa Maria Liberatrice. In the middle distance stand the three remaining columns of the Temple of Castor and Pollux, consecrated in 484 BC, and next to them, the fountain that provided water for the cattle market. Beyond this, at the left, is the portico of the Temple of Faustina of AD 141 within which is the church of San Lorenzo in Miranda, erected in the twelfth century and completed in 1602. To the right of these are the Torre delle Milizie and the three colossal arches of the Basilica of Constantine.

The left-hand side of the composition is more imaginary, though it does depict Bernini's *Fountain of the Four Rivers* on the Piazza Navona, which was completed in 1651, and a porphyry sarcophagus that stood in front of the Pantheon until 1666 and is now in the Corsini Chapel of San Giovanni in Laterano. The church at the left, approached by a long flight of steps, cannot be identified, though it forms an obvious complement to that of Sta Maria in Aracoeli in Breenbergh's picture.

Lingelbach was born in Frankfurt in 1622, but in 1634 his family settled in Amsterdam, where he presumably served his apprenticeship as a painter. He is recorded in Rome between 1647 and 1649 and left the city by 1650, returning to Amsterdam, where he is documented in 1653 and remained for the rest of his life. He specialised in anecdotal genre scenes based on his Italian visit and featuring gnome-like figures that are considerably less ambitious or expressive than those of Breenbergh's final years. Given the disparities in scale between the works by the two artists, any putative relationship between them must be regarded as somewhat *ad hoc*. Within Lingelbach's own career, however, the *View of the Forum Romanum* - with its lively brushwork and animated figures - ranks among his undisputed masterpieces.

References: Wildenstein and Co., Ltd., London, *Artists in 17th century Rome*, 1955, p. 64, no. 54; Catja Burger-Wegener, *Johannes Lingelbach 1622-1674*, doctoral dissertation, Free University, Berlin, 1976, pp. 66-7, 106, and 232, no. 24; R1981, p. 90, no. 234; sale Christie's, London, 14 June 2002, p. 152, no. 605.

Fig. 27 (No. 10), Johannes Lingelbach, *View of the Forum Romanum*, 1656,
Private Collection, Europe

11 *Joseph distributing corn in Egypt,* 1669,
by Ferdinand Bol (1616-80)
Inscribed lower right: FBol; 1669
Oil on canvas, 157 x 171 cm.
De Nieuwe Kerk, Amsterdam

During the 1650s and '60s, Dutch history painters turned increasingly to Flemish models for inspiration, above all the works of Rubens, van Dyck and their followers. This is the style that prevailed in the pictures executed to decorate the new Town Hall in Amsterdam during these years by (among others) Ferdinand Bol.

Born in Dordrecht, Bol became one of Rembrandt's most successful pupils of the mid-1630s, painting portraits and history pictures that were heavily indebted to those of his master. By the early 1640s he had established himself as an independent painter in Amsterdam, where he lived for the rest of his life and received many important commissions, among them those for two versions of *Joseph distributing corn in Egypt* of c. 1655 and 1669, the latter of which is exhibited here.[1] By this time he had repudiated the personal manner of Rembrandt in favour of a more international and classical style which is rich in blandishments for the eye and largely undemanding on the mind.

Bol's *Joseph* may instructively be compared with those of Breenbergh as a measure of the degree to which the latter must have appeared an outmoded and eccentric master to many of his contemporaries. Gone now are the scenes of human charity, the livestock, supernumeraries, and Roman and Egyptian landmarks of Breenbergh's imagination. In their place is a group of well-dressed Egyptians offering precious vessels to Joseph in return for corn, like an aristocracy suddenly having fallen upon hard times. In the grandiloquent gestures and billowing draperies of Bol's figures one witnesses the extent to which Breenbergh's cryptic pictorial language has been

superseded by one which is immediately accessible. Thus, whereas the latter's composition is wilfully episodic and divides itself into smaller, self-contained units in the manner of a jig-saw puzzle, that by Bol contains a single focus - Joseph - whose commanding presence acts as a magnet for the rest of the group.

Was Bol aware of Breenbergh's much quirkier treatments of this theme? One may never know for sure. But the presence in the younger artist's pictures of a man struggling to carry a portion of grain, his forehead bulging and knotted and his back turned to the main group, suggests a clear relationship between the two. Yet another is the man at the margins of all three pictures bearing a sack of grain on his head.

But in what direction did the influence flow - Bol to Breenbergh or Breenbergh to Bol? Given the fact that Bol's earlier version of this theme dates from the mid-1650s, one cannot be certain. But what can be said is that the exertions of both of these figures are much more in keeping with the highly-strung world of Breenbergh than the blander and more conventional one of Bol. If this is the case, then the latter-day Pre-Rembrandtist - by now decidedly out of fashion - would still appear to have had something to teach the younger generation.

1 For the version of c. 1655, see A. Blankert, *Ferdinand Bol, 1616-80,* Doornspijk and Groningen, 1982, p. 95, no. 13 (wrongly identified there, along with the present picture, as *Bringing Gifts for the Temple of Solomon*).

References: A. Blankert, *Ferdinand Bol, 1616-80,* Doornspijk and Groningen, 1982, p. 95, no. 12; Westfälisches Landesmuseum, *Im Lichte Rembrandts, Das Alte Testament im Goldenen Zeitalter der niederländischen Kunst,* 1994, p. 253, no. 27.

Fig. 28 (No. 11), Ferdinand Bol, *Joseph distributing corn in Egypt*, 1669, De Nieuwe Kerk, Amsterdam

Drawings

Bartholomeus Breenbergh

12 *The Torre di Chia,* c. 1624
Pen and brown ink, grey and brown wash,
over black chalk, 39.5 x 52.3 cm.
Day & Faber, London

The Torre di Chia, located 6 km south of Bomarzo, where Breenbergh often worked during his Italian years (cf. cat. 13), was a fiefdom of the Orsini family. It forms the subject of four drawings and one painting attributable to the artist.[1] The present work is the largest of them all and is datable to c. 1624. Another version, in the Hermitage, actually bears this date. The prominent fold in the centre of the sheet indicates that it once formed part of an album or sketchbook. Though the drawing is twice inscribed on the reverse with the name of Jan de Bisschop - one of the artist's major followers (cf. cat. 24 and 25) - it is now widely attributed to Breenbergh himself and regarded as the prime version of this subject to survive by the artist, a view which may be further assessed in the present exhibition.[2] Unquestionably, it possesses a fluency and spontaneity - together with a preliminary chalk underdrawing - unique to this version, that would argue strongly in favour of such a view.

The technique of the drawing - with its black chalk underdrawing, energetic pen work and freely-applied washes - is characteristic of Breenbergh's landscape sketches throughout his career and distinguishes them from comparable works by his Italian predecessors and contemporaries, such as Annibale Carracci (1560-1609) and Domenichino (1581-1641), whose nature studies are invariably executed in pen or chalk alone.

1 For the others, see R1969, p. 23, nos. 13 and 14 and R1991, p. 83, fig. 13 and p. 93.
2 Sold as Breenbergh in 1982 (Christie's, London, 23 March, lot 68), the drawing's authenticity was nonetheless questioned by Marcel Roethlisberg (*sic*), 'New Works by Bartholomeus Breenbergh', *Oud Holland*, vol. 99, 1985, p. 66, no. 19.

Reference: Day and Faber, London, *Works on Paper*, 2004, pp. 18-19, no. 8.

Fig. 29 (No. 12), Bartholomeus Breenbergh, *The Torre di Chia*, Day & Faber, London

13 *The Fountain of Pegasus at Bomarzo,* 1625
Inscribed lower right: Bart.° breenbergh f. a. Roma. 1625
Pen and brown wash, 50.4 x 28 cm.
The British Museum, London

An undisputed masterpiece among Breenbergh's landscape drawings, this work reveals the freshness, spontaneity and subtlety of his art - even (as appears here) when he was working from memory. The inscription indicates that this drawing was made in Rome, though it depicts a site to the north of the city, in the garden of Bomarzo, near Bracciano. In the artist's lifetime this area was ruled by the Orsini, Dukes of Bracciano, and it is likely that he worked for Paolo Giordano Orsini II.

The fountain of the winged horse Pegasus was one of a number that adorned the family's park at Bomarzo. Erected c. 1522, it is depicted here framed by clumps of trees rendered with a vigour and virtuosity that are characteristic of the artist's finest nature studies. In the centre the cascading waters of the fountain fall onto a bed of rock.

This magnificent sheet was bequeathed to the British Museum in 1824 by the celebrated English connoisseur and collector, Richard Payne Knight (1751-1824); and it exists in two other, smaller versions by a later hand. The motif of the Fountain of Pegasus was also incorporated by Breenbergh into two paintings of 1633 and 1640 depicting the theme of Cimone and Ifigenia from Boccaccio's *Decameron*.[1]

1 R1981, p. 63, no. 147; p. 78, no. 198.

References: Hind 1926, p. 57, no. 8; R1969, pp. 28-9, no. 41; Rijksmuseum, Amsterdam, *Drawn to Warmth, 17th century Dutch artists in Italy*, by Peter Schatborn, 2001, pp. 67-71.

Fig. 30 (No. 13), Bartholomeus Breenbergh, *The Fountain of Pegasus at Bomarzo*, 1625, The British Museum, London

14 *Old House,* c. 1625
Pen and brown wash, 11.4 x 8.5 cm.
The British Museum, London

A characteristic study of Breenbergh's Italian years, this drawing focuses upon an oblique view of an old house, its weathered features enlivened by a bold play of light and shade. It is the only surviving work by Breenbergh to have furnished a model for one of twelve engravings of antique ruins after the artist, issued by the obscure printmaker, M. Schaep, in 1648 - a measure of how substantial may be the losses among his drawings.

Along with cat. 15-21, this was one of eight works by Breenbergh purchased for the nation in 1836 from the collection of the Yorkshire cloth manufacturer, John Sheepshanks (1787-1863) whose bequest of English paintings to the South Kensington Museum (now the Victoria and Albert Museum) was intended to form the basis of a National Gallery of British Art. His collection of works on paper - which comprised 7,666 prints and 812 drawings - was acquired for £5,000, the entire purchase price funded by a Treasury grant after a lengthy process of lobbying by the Trustees of the British Museum, supported by no less than thirty-seven artists, including Cotman and Landseer.

Reference: Hind 1926, p. 58, no. 12; R1969, p. 31, no. 57.

Fig. 31 (No. 14), Bartholomeus Breenbergh, *Old House*, The British Museum, London

Fig. 32 (No. 15), Bartholomeus Breenbergh, *Group of Houses on a Rocky Outcrop*, The British Museum, London

15 *Group of Houses on a Rocky Outcrop,* c. 1626
Inscribed lower right: BB. fecit
Pen and brown wash, 6.7 x 12.4 cm.
The British Museum, London

Breenbergh's predilection for antique ruins and dilapidated buildings is one of the trademarks of his art, and this striking sheet is no exception. Like the preceding drawing, this focuses upon its subject seen at an angle, its picturesque qualities enhanced by the bold play of washes that animate the group of houses and surrounding terrain.

Along with a large number of Breenbergh's other landscape drawings from his Italian years, this work is signed, suggesting that it may have had commercial value.

Reference: Hind 1926, p. 58, no. 11; R1969, p. 31, no. 58.

16 *Palace and Ruins,* c. 1627
  Inscribed lower left: BB. f.
  Pen and grey wash, 9.3 x 15.1 cm.
  The British Museum, London

This is one of two surviving versions of this motif by the artist. The other, in the Louvre, is slightly smaller and lacks the striking tonal contrasts of the present drawing.[1] Though dating from Breenbergh's years in Italy, c. 1627, it was later re-employed in the background of a landscape with Atalante and Hippomenes of 1630 (Staatliche Kunstsammlungen, Kassel), which almost certainly dates from after the artist's return to the Netherlands.[2]

1   R1969, p. 35, no. 80.
2   R1981, pp. 58-9, no. 133.

References: Hind, 1926, p. 58; R1969, p. 34, no. 79.

Fig. 33 (No. 16), Bartholomeus Breenbergh, *Palace and Ruins*, The British Museum, London

Fig. 34 (No. 17), Bartholomeus Breenbergh, *The Tomb of the Plautii*, The British Museum, London

17 *The Tomb of the Plautii,* c. 1627
  Inscribed lower right: BBreenbergh
  Pen and brown wash, 8.5 x 12.5 cm.
  The British Museum, London

The tomb of the Plautii is located alongside the Ponte Lucano, which spans the River Anio (or Aniene), near Tivoli, to the north-east of Rome. It was erected by M Plautius Silvanus, consul to the Emperor Augustus in 2 BC, who died between AD 10 and 14. Inscriptions on the tomb indicate that it was still in use in AD 79, but it was despoiled in the Middle Ages. In 1465, Pope Paul II added a parapet to it and it has largely remained in this state ever since.

Breenbergh's drawing contains an inscription on the reverse identifying the site, and is the artist's only surviving study of this motif.

Reference: Hind 1926, p. 58, no. 13; R1969, p. 35, no. 81.

Fig. 35 (No. 18), Bartholomeus Breenbergh, *In the Colosseum*, The British Museum, London

18 *In the Colosseum,* c. 1628.
   Inscribed lower left: BB f.
   Pen and grey wash, 9 x 14.7 cm.
   The British Museum, London

The Colosseum, the most famous monument of ancient Rome, figures prominently in Breenbergh's paintings and drawings and forms the subject of one of the latter as late as 1639, when the artist had been back in the Netherlands for a decade.[1] This is one of his many views of the building, seen from within, and once formed part of a sketchbook, hence the page number 35 at the upper right.

1 R1969, p. 47, no. 147.

References: Hind 1926, p. 58, no. 15; R1969, p. 35, no. 82.

Fig. 36 (No. 19), Bartholomeus Breenbergh, *The Bridge at Ostia*, The British Museum, London

19 *The Bridge at Ostia,* c. 1628

Inscribed centre left: BB f.
Black chalk and brown wash, 26.6 x 39 cm.
The British Museum, London

Purportedly depicting a bridge near Ostia, to the south-west of Rome, this striking landscape study is datable to the end of Breenbergh's Italian years, c. 1628, and was evidently made as a work of art in its own right. Yet it was subsequently re-used by the artist for a painting of *Christ healing the Blind* which dates from the early 1630s and depicts the dome of the Cathedral at Florence under the arch of the bridge[1] - a salutary reminder of the extent to which Breenbergh exercised his imagination when portraying architectural settings. Particularly notable about the present sheet is the seated man, seen from behind, contemplating the site at the edge of the river-bank, who anticipates countless comparable figures of the neo-classical and romantic periods, awestruck by the grandeur of ancient Rome.

1 R1981, p. 67, no. 162.

References: Hind 1926, p. 57, no. 9; R1969, p. 38, no. 103.

Fig. 37 (No. 20), Bartholomeus Breenbergh, *Ruins*, The British Museum, London

20 *Ruins*, c. 1625
   Pen with brown and grey wash, 22.1 x 39.9 cm.
   The British Museum, London

Roethlisberger has plausibly suggested that the subject of this magnificent drawing may be the foundations of an ancient thermal bath. In its lively pen-work and variegated play of washes it demonstrates the extraordinary dexterity of Breenbergh's nature studies and ranks among the finest of all his landscape drawings.

References: Hind 1926, p. 57, no. 10; R1969, p. 39, no. 105.

60

Fig. 38 (No. 21), Bartholomeus Breenbergh, *San Gregorio Magno*, The British Museum, London

21 *San Gregorio Magno,* c. 1628

Pen with brown and grey wash, 8.7 x 15.2 cm.
The British Museum, London

Even if this drawing had not survived, it would be reasonable to suppose that Breenbergh had been familiar with the church of San Gregorio Magno in Rome, since one of its most famous works of art - Guido Reni's fresco of *St Andrew led to his Martyrdom* (fig. 16) - furnished the motif for the striking young woman, regally clad, who is depicted tipping a coin into the hands of a young beggar-boy at the left of his two late versions of *Joseph distributing corn in Egypt*. Originally dating from the medieval period, and substantially altered in the seventeenth and eighteenth centuries, the church is here shown from the rear, its picturesque qualities evidently much more important to Breenbergh than its architectural features.

References: Hind 1926, p. 58, no. 14; R1969, p. 40, no. 110.

61

Fig. 39 (No. 22), Bartholomeus Breenbergh, *Architectural Fantasy*, The British Museum, London

22 *Architectural Fantasy,* c. 1640

Graphite and pen with grey wash, 14.2 x 15.6 cm.
The British Museum, London

Clearly conceived as a work of art in its own right, this evocative architectural caprice dates from long after Breenbergh had returned from Italy, c. 1640, and anticipates the two late versions of *Joseph distributing corn in Egypt* in its heady mixture of motifs, the column at the left, the ruins and rusticated buildings combined to simulate an operatic stage set. Adding to its sense of fantasy and mystery is the fleeing figure of a man at the right, who appears to be about to descend the flight of steps, as though determined to make a quick escape. With its ominous shadows and air of lurking menace, the scene anticipates the haunted cityscapes of Giorgio de Chirico of the 1910s and remains one of Breenbergh's rare imaginary landscape drawings.

References: Hind 1926, p. 58, no. 17; R1969, p. 44, no. 136.

Fig. 40 (No. 23), Bartholomeus Breenbergh, *Joseph distributing corn in Egypt*, Belasting & Douane Museum, Rotterdam, The Netherlands

Prints

23 ***Joseph distributing corn in Egypt,*** c. 1645
   Etching, 46.6 x 68.2 cm. borderline; 50.7 x 69.3 cm. plate
   Belasting & Douane Museum, Rotterdam,
   The Netherlands

24 ***Joseph distributing corn in Egypt,*** c. 1655
   Jan de Bisschop (1628-71), after Breenbergh
   (illustrated overleaf)
   Etching, 45.3 x 66.9 cm.
   The British Museum, London

Breenbergh's 1644 version of *Joseph distributing corn in Egypt* was the subject of countless copies, imitations, and reproductive prints. These two etchings are among the earliest examples of such works. The first was executed by Breenbergh himself and is his largest etching, its size and quality attesting to the fact that the artist set great store by the composition. The second is by the draughtsman and etcher, Jan de Bisschop, who is widely assumed to have been Breenbergh's pupil and was certainly his most devoted follower (cf. cat. 7 and 25). Born in Amsterdam in

Fig. 41 (No. 24), Jan de Bisschop (after Breenbergh), *Joseph distributing corn in Egypt*, The British Museum, London

1628, de Bisschop eventually founded a drawing academy in The Hague, where he died prematurely in 1671.

Both etchings are in the same sense as Breenbergh's original painting and follow it very closely; and it is presumed that de Bisschop's etching was made after that of the master, rather than from the original canvas. It includes a Latin inscription below which reads: 'There was a famine in the land of Canaan. And Joseph was governor in Egypt, and at his command corn was sold to the people. Gen. 42.6. The Governor is the image and exemplar of God on earth, the moderator and arbiter of deeds, in whose hands wealth, dignity, and life are put. Lipsius *De una religione Liber* (1591).' The reference is to a treatise by the notable Flemish humanist and philosopher, Justus Lipsius (1547-1606).

Breenbergh's etching appears to be the last he executed after one of his works, though de Bisschop was to make another, after the *Martyrdom of St Lawrence* of 1647 (cat. 25). What prompted the master to undertake this task will never be known. But there can be little doubt that it helped clinch the position of the 1644 *Joseph distributing corn in Egypt* as his most celebrated work.

References: F. W. H. Hollstein, *Dutch and Flemish Etchings, Engravings and Woodcuts ca. 1450 - 1700*, Amsterdam, 1949, II, p. 42, no. 1 and III, p. 213, no. 30; R1981, pp. 80-2, no. 204. (de Bisschop only); Peter van der Coelen, *Patriarchs, Angels & Prophets, The Old Testament in Netherlandish Printmaking from Lucas van Leyden to Rembrandt*, Rembrandthuis, Amsterdam, 1996, pp. 95-6, no. 20.

Fig. 42 (No. 25), Jan de Bisschop (after Breenbergh), *The Martyrdom of St Lawrence*, The British Museum, London

25 *The Martyrdom of St Lawrence,* c. 1650

Jan de Bisschop (1628-71), after Breenbergh
Etching, 45.5 x 68 cm.
The British Museum, London

One of two reproductive etchings after Breenbergh by de Bisschop (cf. cat. 24), this is based (in reverse) on the former's painting of 1647 (cat. 9), though with significant changes. The tree at the left of the original canvas has been omitted and the column that appears alongside it has been replaced by a statue of Jupiter, enthroned and addressing the populace, as though to reinforce the pagan worship which has led to the saint's undoing.

The print is inscribed below: 'While the blessed Lawrence was burning, chained down over the faggots, he said to the most wicked tyrant, "The roast is done [this side]; now turn it over and then devour it. For the hands of the poor have carried away the wealth of the Church, which you are seeking, to heavenly treasure-stores." Just as Jerusalem was glorified by Stephen, so was Rome made illustrious by Lawrence.'

References: F. W. H. Hollstein, *Dutch and Flemish Etchings, Engravings and Woodcuts ca. 1450 - 1700*, Amsterdam, 1949, II, p. 43, no. 3; R1981, p. 89, no. 228.

Fig. 43 (No. 26), Cornelis Cort (after Titian), *The Martyrdom of St Lawrence*, 1571, The British Museum, London

26 ***The Martyrdom of St Lawrence,*** 1571
Cornelis Cort (c. 1533-78), after Titian
Engraving, 48.5 x 34 cm.
The British Museum, London

In the latter half of his career, Titian painted two astonishing altarpieces of the Martyrdom of St Lawrence, one for the church of the Gesuiti in Venice (1548-57) and the other for Philip II of Spain (Escorial; c. 1567). Unquestionably the greatest of all treatments of this theme, these two works became best-known through this magnificent engraving, which combines elements from both compositions and was presumably designed especially by the painter for the Netherlandish engraver, Cornelis Cort, resident in Italy since 1565, to work from.

The print probably provided the basis for Breenbergh's canvas of this scene (cat. 9), which bears obvious similarities to it in the position of the saint on the grill, the executioners attacking him, and the antique statue above. But whereas Titian creates a scene of universal drama and pathos in which all of the figures are focused upon the saint in a unified and concerted action, Breenbergh depicts a more haphazard and uncoordinated scene. As in the two late versions of *Joseph distributing corn in Egypt*, the Dutch master's solution resembles a dress rehearsal for the subject rather than a well-drilled performance.

References: M. Sellink, *The New Hollstein, Dutch and Flemish Etchings, Engravings and Woodcuts, 1450 - 1700: Cornelis Cort*, Rotterdam, 2000, II, p. 176, no. 126; Michael Bury, *The Print in Italy 1550 - 1620*, London, British Museum Press, 2001, p. 92, no. 56.

Selected Bibliography

Andrews, Keith, *Adam Elsheimer*, Oxford, 1977.

Bauch, Kurt, 'Beiträge zum Werk der Vorläufer Rembrandts, I. Die Gemälde des Jan Pynas', *Oud Holland*, LII, 1935, pp. 145-58.

Blankert, Albert, *Nederlandse 17e Eeuwe Italianiserende Landschapschilders*, Soest, 1978.

Dézaillier d'Argenville, A., *Abrégé de la vie des plus fameux peintres...*, Paris, 1762, III, pp. 148-50.

Duparc, Frederik J. and Linda L. Graif, *Italian Recollections, Dutch Painters of the Golden Age*, The Montreal Museum of Fine Arts, 1990.

Harwood, Laurie B., *Inspired by Italy, Dutch Landscape Painting 1600-1700*, Dulwich Picture Gallery, 2002.

Hind, Arthur M., *Catalogue of Drawings by Dutch and Flemish Artists...in the British Museum*, III (A-M), London, 1926.

Nalis, Door H. J., 'Bartholomeus Breenbergh', *Vereeniging tot Beofening van Overijsselsch Regt en Geschiedenis, Verslagen en Mededelingen*, Kampen, 1972, pp. 62-81.

Nalis, Door H. J., 'Bartholomeus Breenbergh', *Vereeniging tot Beofening van Overijsselsch Regt en Geschiedenis, Verslagen en Mededelingen*, Zwolle, 1973, pp. 51-9.

Roethlisberger, Marcel, *Bartholomäus Breenbergh, Handzeichnungen*, Berlin, 1969.

Roethlisberger, Marcel, *Bartholomeus Breenbergh, The Paintings*, Berlin and New York, 1981.

Roethlisberger, Marcel, 'New Works by Bartholomeus Breenbergh', *Oud Holland*, Vol. 99, 1985, pp. 57-66.

Roethlisberger, Marcel George, *Bartholomeus Breenbergh*, Richard L. Feigen & Company, London, 1991.

Schatborn, Peter, *Drawn to Warmth, 17th Century Dutch Artists in Italy*, Rijksmuseum, Amsterdam, 2001.

Sluijter-Seiffert, Nicolette C., 'Bartholomeus Breenbergh', *The Dictionary of Art*, London, 1996, IV, pp. 733-5.

Stechow, Wolfgang, 'Bartholomeus Breenbergh, Landschafts- und Historienmaler', *Jahrbuch der Preuszischen Kunstsammlungen*, LI, 1930, pp. 133-40.

Tümpel, Astrid, *The Pre-Rembrandtists*, E. B. Crocker Art Gallery, Sacramento, 1974.

Tümpel, Astrid, 'Claes Cornelisz. Moeyaert', *Oud Holland*, Vol. 88, 1974, pp. 1-163.

Tümpel, Astrid and Peter Schatborn, *Pieter Lastman, the man who taught Rembrandt*, Rembrandthuis, Amsterdam, 1991.

Tümpel, Christian and others, *Im Lichte Rembrandts, Das Alte Testament im Goldenen Zeitalter der niederländischen Kunst*, Westfälisches Landesmuseum, Münster, 1994.

Photo Credits